CONTENTS

EDITORIAL

Could modernity and its technologies save much of rural Scotland from turning into a depopulated backwater? It was a question that occupied some of the great minds of the 20th century – like Patrick Geddes, and as Frances Robertson shows us, Hugh MacDiarmid. The whole notion of an 'electric pastorale' is evident paradox – but what were to be its long term effects? Robertson tells us of 'a nest of concepts about place, nation, and identity that are far too complex to be laughed off as mere false consciousness.'

Does modernity change a place only for the better, and irreversibly at that? Or is the long run prospect one of the creation of 'heritage' where once 'culture' had deep roots? The density in Raymond Burke's stories may seem only obliquely related here – but his fearful and suspicious inhabitants of a central belt New Town would surely suggest that the great modernist tabula rasa experiment in creating new urban communities was a particular type of rebirth that was not without its traumas.

Perhaps that dismissive notion of 'false consciousness' is indeed an everyday phenomenon, unavoidable in our deracinated world of 'heritage'? It's surely a truism, after all, that many mod Scots find the toes curl at mere mention of the word 'clan'. It may well be thoroughly bedded down in many highland locations in Robertson's 'nest of concepts' but does it not immediately conjure up –in arms length inverted commas – images of 'Homecomings', of 'Gatherings', and posh Highland 'chieftains' in expensive brogues and polished English or American accents? What could that have to do with any 'real life' identity? The mind boggles (not falsely) at the question, but as Mitch Miller relates, the artist Ross Sinclair brandishes his body in that debate. Yet he does it in a kindly and innocent way, he gets physically close to people to open up the question of that 'nest of concepts' , and allows for a construction of a 'jerry-built clan… surprisingly dissonant and inclusive'.

And it's with the re-opening of a connection between identity and memory that Steve Davsimoon also wants to talk to us about particular places. He also wants a body to make those connections – to come close and listen to the real life of place in sound. That's music.

JR

"Times may change quoth the great prophet" Connolly (Billy), "But standards must remain."

Connolly of course, meant the correct deportment of airline pilots ("Moustache, epaulets, ciggies in the top pocket, trousers"). In pre-Referendum Scotland that sneery and above-mentioned dismissal of 'false consciousness' is a standard that remains against which Labour hacks, Gorgeous George Galloway and die-hard, pure-as-the-driven anarchists find the likes of National Collective wanting.

Because of course, progressive politics can only take place within the guidelines of a united kingdom. Or Ireland. Or abroad. No doubt the young activists of the 'National Collective' have a poor grasp of the dialectic, but up close and sharing their space, Andrew Tickell discovers plenty of healthy admixture and alloy among this group, less 'Wha's like us' and more 'Scotland – whit like is it?'

Times do change; back when Owen Dudley Edwards was a hipster, could anyone envisage a vote on dismantling the British state, or equal marriage for gay and lesbian couples? Sometimes, Owen Dudley Edwards tells us, one has to proclaim independence and wait for everyone else to catch up. He goes on to explain how Ian Rankin is a literary craftsman and political artist on a par with Florentine masters such as Machiavelli, and Scottish Tory Leader Ruth Davidson was the existential hero of the equal marriage debate (even as she is trapped by other forms of eternal union).

We at The Drouth share widespread concerns that the BBC will bar Doctor Who from an independent Scotland. So while we are still able to use him as a subpar literary device, we must ask – if an (exiled) Peter Capaldi kidnapped a Scottish citizen en route to the polling station in 1979, and then plonk them here in 2014, would they actually recognise Scotland in either its substance or surface?

By designing pitheads in Monktonhall, Seafield, Bilston Glen and Kiloch, Hungarian designer Egon Riss arguably did more to shape the standard image of both. There is perhaps too much macro in the micro of Johnny Rodger's rueful judgement that his reputation has diminished to 'a mere dabbler in dinky interior design' for our liking – the complete eradication of all material evidence of Riss' designs along with the industries he served consigns a swathe of our history to textual lacunae and physical gapsites.

But about those airline pilots, or rather, the industry they serve. Rachel Gannon's Being There explores airports as 'non-places', where the surface really is the substance. By drawing in situ, Gannon works against the grain of these carefully engineered voids (almost you could say, as some sort of impurity). Her fluid, quirky line chronicles the time it took to make it, and thus, finds history exactly where we least expect it.

MM

Andrew Tickell

IN THE HIPSTERS' DEN

:the playful politics of #IndyRef

Country: Scotland. Whit like is it? It's a peatbog, it's a daurk forest. It's a hipster's den. A raided vintage shop. *It's a cauldron o' lye, a saltpan or a coal mine.* A Teddy boy flailing against a foliage of iPhones, every leaf winking bright. Swank German beer. Earnest, spoken word poetry and safe, self-penned acoustic strumming. Rolled-up fags and asymmetric haircuts and ironic tweed. *It's a tenement or a merchant's ha'.* A cobbled street, saltires burling. It's anti-folk post-rock. The broken back of an incomplete monument to Nelson. Loki's Glaswegian hip-hop with an independent message. Grey men with grey plans for the nation, old familiars we can't seem to displace. It's a march or a hoolie; a meeting or a conversation. Sober *or* playful, serious *and* playful. *It depends. It depends...*

It was quite something. *Mono* was already crammed when Liz Lochhead was field-promoted onto the billing. It didn't take much coaxing to convince the Scottish Makar to totter up to mic. "Would you do the Corbie's speech? From *Mary Queen of Scots Got Her Head Chopped Off*"? In the flesh, she's wee. The general hubbub didn't subside – at least not initially – but within a few lines, a shoosh enveloped the whole room. *"Ah dinna ken whit like your Scotland is. Here 'smines. National flower: the thistle. National pastime: nostalgia."*

Nothing about the setting recalled the *la recherche du temps perdu*. If your understanding of Scotland's constitutional debate is based solely on BBC *Newsnicht's* Gothic night-life of elderly gentlemen howling partisan talking points past each other, or the bloodless columns and articles of the mainstream press, you could be forgiven for seeing the referendum campaign as just another talking point in the ashen, exclusive work of political business as usual. But unreported, beneath the headlines about currency policy, technical EU membership rules and future pension provision, a new wealth of social connections are springing up around this referendum. Come a Yes vote *or* a No vote on the 18th of September 2014, these new ties, these friendships and comradeships, these self-confident, self-organised solidarities will stay with us.

National Collective represents just one outpost of Scotland's new political sociability. Conceived as a locus for pro-independence "artists and creatives" – I cringed at first too – this is something of a misnomer. While National Collective includes a smattering of established playwrights, poets, architects and designers within their ranks – if the crowd at their Glasgow launch was anything to go by, it is really the youth outpost of Yes Scotland, incorporating folk vaguely interested in creativity and culture, but unified most by their generational ties and a shared constitutional vision. And none the worse for that. Surveying the convivial crowd, the coruscating lights, the music, the poetry, supping a pint, one young man observed, mordantly: "I thought this is what politics would be like when I joined the Greens."

He had in mind the more usual unrefreshed political fare of stuffing envelopes, being shooed off by cantankerous pensioners, maintaining your grin as you canvass the racist voter who supports your candidate, of vaulting up closes and scaling tenements and towers, weary and out of puff. This was certainly different. As the group's co-founder Ross Colquhoun observes, with National Collective, "politics seems fun again." The strapline of movement's recent launch at Edinburgh's Wee Red Bar sums up the spirit. Echoing and adapting the aspirational dictum popularised by Alasdair Gray, "come party as if you lived in the early days of a better nation!"

But for the Scottish accents, we could have been anywhere from a college bar in New England to a self-conscious Melbourne coffee shop. Skinny jeans, stringy undergraduates, narrow-beamed boys in lumberjack red, girls in Scandinavian knits and embroidered oriental house coats; geometric specs in tortoise-shell and a higher than average beard-count: hipsterism rampant. There were even a few self-conscious '80s power-shouldered suits. And, here and there, a few stray pickled old socialists with pints of heavy, who have forgone the Trot's faith in a red world, propounding the rather more modest slogan "Another Scotland is Possible". *National weather: smirr, haar, drizzle, snow* – Liz gave it laldy and the patchwork young crowd of post-modern fragments hushed up.

The enveloping stillness was no accident, and no politeness. The hush was generational and sincere. Most of the folk hubbubing about must have been born after Lochhead's 1987 play was first written, but almost all of them seemed to know it well. Having been educated in one of those private bastions of the Glaswegian bourgeoisie during the late 1990s and early 2000s, which exposed us to almost no Scottish literature (or even Scottish history), I came to Liz Lochhead's work late, on my own initiative, at university. For most of the crowd, however, it formed a cornerstone of their secondary education in the literature of their own country. Not unalloyed happy connotations, perhaps, but a seminal text for this generation, and here, on stage, its author barks out this memorable passage with gusto to a group of young Scots, enjoying the revels, united by nothing save their aspirations for Scotland's constitutional future.

It isn't a moment which conjures headlines, but it is an unusual experience in Scotland of what politics can and might mean. Our under-resourced national media, with its fleeting attention span, fixation on the fortunes of leading figures and party outfits, and demand for newsworthy and sudden reversals, is poorly placed to track gradual developments in our politics.

For many supporters of independence, the perceived biases of the Scottish media represent their biggest, growling bugbear about this campaign. For me, the reality is sadder, and more impoverishing. We live in a marvellous, rich, lively, complex, humane country. A land marked with its share of griefs and follies, to be sure – what place is otherwise? – but a Scotland with a multiform pied beauty, a couple-colour which is "counter, original, spare, strange." You rarely encounter that busy, many-peopled Scotland in our waning newspaper typeface, or in our flyblown, cash-strapped and overcautious broadcasting studios.

But when you've an eye only for earthquakes and eruptions, the slow drift of the tectonic plates too often goes undetected. Like most economic prophets of our time, the vision of Scotland's political seers too often have proved faulty. The annihilation of the Scottish Labour Party in 2011 by the SNP caught everyone by surprise. Jack McConnell's narrower defeat in 2007 less so, perhaps, but its consequences were largely unforeseen.

I wonder if the same isn't true about this referendum campaign. In and of itself, a cheery night getting lushed up with the politically like-minded changes nothing. For cynics, this may smack of preaching to the converted rather than reaching the undecided. Pints and pints, however pristine their craft micro-brewed credentials, don't shift minds from No to Yes. But they do form connections, introducing a whole generation of would-be active citizens to one other, united around a shared goal. In a wee country like ours, such movements are not to be underestimated.

Despite the apparently limitless surety and security of the Powers that Be, in a circumscribed community, a knot of committed citizens with a plan and a will can change the world. And missionary morale is always important. Like the Radical Independence Conferences of this November and last, it is difficult to imagine this gathering's shadow – the bright night when a band of committed young folk committed to continuing Union assemble and organise themselves, and ask: what can we do to build up a movement, to change our nation for the better?

It is also a striking rebuke to the self-serving story of the satiated baby-boomer, whose politics have plundered the national estate, and whose political imagination is haunted by visions of a disreputable, idle youth who deserve the economic disaffection and financial deprivation and uncertainty to which many of us have been consigned. For some of you, the bustling room I have just described will recall the torments and horrors of the tenth ring of hell Dante forgot, reserved for the poseurings and affectations of wanky youth. But it is the lot of every generation to denigrate the fashions of their successors, and I'd encourage you to take a second look.

Even for those chock full of green sap and optimism, it is quite something, to emerge into a world in which you can expect a worse standard of living than your parents all the way down the line, and worse, to be blamed for falling foul of the ruthless economic circumstances which you have done nothing to foster. It isn't a cockle-warming tale to tell, that of this lost generation. Yet the folk I meet are not sinking into a joyless oblivion of emptying intoxication and distraction. Their political and creative impulses are stimulated, not depressed, by these circumstances. The vision may not be programmatic, or governmental – not yet – but only the sourest spirit could believe that the only legitimate driver behind a generation rediscovering the possibilities of active citizenship is a belt-and-braces conception of policy and statecraft. If the precondition is a little fun along the way, *honi soit qui mal y pense*.

Despite being bludgeoned flat by the recession, opportunities constricted, prospects curtailed, on their own initiative, this band of young folk decided to try to make a difference, and contribute to the great debate on the future of their country. Not as a calculated way-station on the course of a personally ambitious political trajectory, taking them from party hack to salaried researcher to unshiftable parliamentarian – but out of a desire to sound in the political sphere, as an end in itself. At bottom, it represents a refusal to be bored into submission.

It also rejects the atomised political Quietism commended by Russell Brand, and the exhaustion with democratic politics, violent imagery and flip cynicism which he represents. The Dickensian breadstick's digressive *New Statesman* diatribe, calling for revolution through inaction, recalled Mark Corrigan of *Peep Show*'s marvellously caustic diagnosis of his flaccid flat-mate, Jeremy: "the absolute worst thing anyone could say about you is that you were a selfish moral blank, whose lazy cynicism and sneering ironic take on the world encapsulates everything wrong with a generation, but you my friend are not evil."

Political problems have political solutions. The idea that things can never change, and are impervious to political agency, is one of our age's worst super-stitions. The young folk I've met in this campaign all repudiate it utterly. It's a common sense which I wish was more common. It may be that their constitutional aspirations are blunted next autumn, and Scotland will remain a stateless nation for at least another generation. Whatever happens, and on whatever side of the argument they fall, this campaign will shape that generation for the better.

There's a distinctively modern flavour to the night's many meetings too. Some of this takes the form of the ghastly phenomenon gripping this generation of photos-of-people-taking-photos – a very contem-porary archival fever, fostered by the ubiquity of the iPhone and an unhealthy obsessive-compulsive impulse that no experience is adequately authenticated without having been documented, and tweeted. On the other hand, a clear-eyed understanding of the power of the image is also at work here. It is important, not only that the event is happening, but that it is *seen* to be happening, and seen to be *happening*.

The internet is indispensable. While social media is not in want of glaikit seers and spiritualists of new age, new-management bollocks who cash in on overstating its influence, it would be wrong I think to see Twitter's endless chirping as an empty hall of masks, without any meaningful connection to "the real world", as some would have it. I'm of that on-the-cusp generation, riding the early wave which popularised mass-computerisation in the early 1990s.

The late Iain Banks' *Wasp Factory* is the period piece which captures this disconnectedness best (though I hasten to add that, even as a macabre rural mite, I did not maintain my own array of Sacrifice Poles). Our modest primary school in rural mid-Argyll boasted only a steam-powered Macintosh and an even more ancient, pixelated piece of kit, whose solitary function seemed to be games of Frogger. So you notice the technological shifts and intrusions, without becoming an elderly and illiterate luddite, who struggles to fiddle anything beyond a fountain pen into functionality.

Many, if not most of the exchanges rippling across the room are not first encounters but the first revisiting in the flesh of familiar folk from online. With strangers, you're often first struck by the gulf of social distance between you. Trying to bridge these unknown unknowns, you footer around clumsily for things in common. This often miscarries. Drinks are sipped awkwardly. You're both grateful for dishonest excuses which disentangle you from the wreck of failed sociability. Neither of you let on.

But Twitter narrows that social distance. You have an instant shared agenda for conversation. Much of the bashfulness is eliminated. It's like the good will attending a friend of a friend. Sometimes, the creature who presents themselves before you differs radically from the persona they have cultivated online. More often, you encounter a rough approximation, more richly detailed, perhaps surprising, but with a sense of pre-existing intimacy between you, somehow fostering dialogue, the friend to good conversation.

There's also a pleasing openness about this sort of playful politics. The orthodox account is that this is a bitter campaign, its rough-hide scarred with innumerable acid-splashes and javelines: not territory for the tender-hearted or the tender-skinned to stray into. I disagree. Although the internet, as always, is too frequently characterised by its snark and recrimination, this referendum might represent a rare opportunity to transcend *some* of the irrational, calcified hatreds which govern too many of our political exchanges in this country.

There's an iteration of our politics which sees Scots as inveterate tribalists. In the late 18th and early 19th centuries, under the douce and watchful attentions of Henry Dundas, Scotland's very sparse electorate were strongly for the Tories and Mr Pitt, A century later, this succeeded to Liberal domination, followed by a Unionist upswing, and most recently, by the long domination of the British Labour Party. Now the SNP and Labour scrap it out with eye-popping and irrational hostility. While the adults comport themselves like children, the kids are a model of civility. Greenies and Labour and SNP supporters natter away with radical young trades unionists and independence-minded Tories, trading views and rounds and laughter. Some of the talk is of politics, but by no means all of it. Gigs, music, films, study, work. The usual. It's a picture of politics interwoven with life. There is no blood on the floor. No dull-eyed party commissar here, ensuring compliance with "the line to take" and executing backsliders. We could do with a little more of that spirit, and a little less unimaginative clannishness and the unreflexive politics of the straw man which it fosters.

Country: Scotland. Whit like is it? Win or lose in 2014, Yes or No, I'm optimistic that this referendum can leave is all strengthened, challenged certainly, but also a generational opportunity to cease tilling the earth with salt. The Corbie's ambivalent Scotland of the 1980s recedes from memory and view. This independence generation is brasher, more assertive, but also unapologetic and unselfconscious in the best, rather traditionally un-Scottish sense. It's a healthy, happy confidence. Cramped *ye cannaes* won't be countenanced. How many generations are afforded the opportunity to answer the question: what kind of country, what kind of democracy do we choose to be? Too many folk are trying to make a banality of that conversation. It still makes my pulse beat faster.

Raymond Burke

CLOSE

Flat 26

Joe sat at the table in the bay window, mistily gazing at the Daily Record, barely scanning each page before flicking on to the next in a slow steady rhythm. He turned his head slightly and looked over his glasses at the dog barking outside the newsagent before resumng his daily disinterest in world events.

When Marion stepped into the living room with some breakfast on a tray, he folded the paper neatly and placed it at the side of the table, glasses on top. Two eggs, one grilled square sausage, one small slice of bacon, two un-fried potato scones and two tablespoons of beans. On a separate plate – two slices of toast – lightly buttered and cut into triangles. It was like a photograph of yesterday's breakfast and every previous day for the past three years. For thirty-five years before that, there would have been more bacon and everything would have been fried together. 'Doctor's orders,' she said for the first few months until he got used to it. Since then breakfast had been precisely the same every day. No matter whether he was on nights or days. Perfectly cooked and presented. Same plates – same tray. She would place it in front of him, return to the kitchen to remove her apron and come back.

'Thanks, darlin',' he would say.

Then she would sit opposite and watch him eat.

'So. How was last night?' she asked.

'Usual. Boring Tuesday. One decent hire into Glasgow about midnight. Think I fell asleep at the rank for a couple of hours. If it wasn't for the school run, I'd have made hee haw.'

'You'll no' sleep the day.'

'I'll get a few hours after we've done the shop. Gets a bit boring sitting there with nothing but the radio.'

'That's what we got you the Kindle for.'

She shoved the plate with the toast on it a few millimetres closer to him.

'Twenty-two's got a new Golf. Saw him leaving in it as I came in,' he informed her.

'Where did he get the money for that? Better no' take our parking space. It's bad enough with that hairdresser's.'

'Maybe he'll get rid of the bike.'

'That monstrosity? Blocking the close. Shouldn't be allowed. Between that and twenty-two's pram. Place is becoming a midden. We never left the pram in the close. Even when we had Charlie. I would always take it up into the flat. Nearly always. Very rarely leave it in the close.'

An hour later, plates cleared and washed, Joe, still seated at the table, was having his second attempt at finding something interesting in the paper. He looked out to watch the ice cream van pull up in front of the shops. Marion got up from the armchair and stood behind him with folded arms.

'Why do we need an ice cream van when we've got a shop?' she asked.

'Dunno.'

'I don't think that swine in the shop's got room for ice cream. Amount of booze he sells. Buckfast by the crate. Don't like him.'

'Cheapest in E.K. apparently.'

'It's a bloody disgrace. Alcohol, tobacco, filthy magazines, lottery tickets and pork pies. I'm a better muslim than him.'

'That's how he can afford the big motors.'

'And flats,' Marion pointed out, before returning to her chair and opening a magazine she hadn't bought from the shop across the street. 'They were playing music again last night. One o'clock nearly.'

Joe turned to look at her. 'Who?'

'They sublets... I think. Her downstairs with the wean.'

'I'll have a word. If I see her.'

Marion smiled. 'I nearly phoned you.'

Joe turned back to the paper. 'But that's not a sublet. That's still council.'

'Across the landing told me we were all owners in here.'

'No. Council. Last one in the street.'

'This used to be a good close. Remember we had the net curtains on the windows? And plants? Old Mr Kennedy used to do the garden until he died. They were all council then. People were much more...'

The intercom buzzed, stopping her in mid-flow.

'Somebody's buzzin'. Who's that?' she asked.

'Never saw anyone walking up the path.'

'Postie's been,' she told him. 'Have a look.'

Joe put his fingertips on the corners of the table and raised himself for a second to get a view of the front door before relaxing back on to his seat and shrugging his shoulders.

'Some bloke. Don't know who it is.'

'What does he want with us?'

'Only one way to find out. Will I get it?'

'No. You stay where you are.'

She got up and stepped into the hall.

'Better not be selling anything,' she said. 'Bloody cheek. You on the nightshift.'

She lifted the handset from the wall. 'Hello?'

A low voice crackled through the small speaker. 'Oh... er... hello. I'm trying to get into number thirty two.

Marion covered the mouthpiece and called over her shoulder towards the living room doorway. 'He's trying to get in to thirty two.'

Joe's reply was a barely audible grunt. She un-covered the mouthpiece. 'This is twenty six.'

'I know. Sorry for disturbing you,' the speaker said.

'Have you tried thirty two?'

'Aye, but there's no answer. Can you buzz me in?'

'We're not supposed to do that.'

'But it's an emergency... I need to deliver something.'

'Emergency? What kind of emergency?'

'It doesny matter. Just gauny open the door?'

'Aye, well, naw. I'm not letting you in.'

The speaker went silent and she hung the handset back on the wall. Almost immediately another buzzer could be heard faintly somewhere else in the building.

Marion popped her head round the frame of the living room door. 'He's trying somebody else.'

The main door to the close was heard slamming shut.

Marion crept back along the hallway and listened. 'Somebody's let him in. He better no come tae this door. I'll phone the polis.'

Joe appeared behind her.

'Get away fae that door,' he told her.

Marion silently waved a hand behind her, signalling him to be quiet. She held her breath and put an eye to the little glass lense.

'Is he coming up the stair?' he asked.

'Ssh!'

After about a minute, Marion crept back towards him and whispered in his ear.

'He's away up the stairs. But he stopped. He stopped on the landing and stared right at me. As if he knew I was looking at him.'

They listened as the doorbell rang upstairs.

Joe led the way back into the living room. 'Just come in here and sit doon.'

They both shuffled into the living room. Joe pretended to return to his paper and Marion sat still, staring to one side and listening intently.

A few minutes passed before three deep thuds echoed through the close.

Rachel Gannon

Being There: Conversational Drawing in a Non-Place

Abstract

Where are we, during the act of drawing, in spirit? (Berger, 2007, p.123)

As an illustrator who uses drawing to make sense of the world this is a particularly pertenent question. I have long been interested in trying to find an answer. To attempt this daunting task I will be reviewing a practice-led project, at the centre of which was a month long drawing residency at London Luton Airport. I worked in-situ at the airport to document and record the space and the travellers (and airport staff) that passed through this self-contained 'non-place' (Augé, 1995) every day. The residency lasted a month, with the singular condition of creating a body of work for display at London Luton Airport. The open remit of this residency meant that I was able to make work that explored my interest in documentary or reportage illustration. This project was guided by practice in the truest sense of the word. It is through the practice or act of drawing and ***being there*** that I have explored the relationship between drawing and space.

> "I seemed to need a new place," she said. "Not necessarily an interesting place. Just a strange place. Without associations. A place where I would be very much alone. Like a hotel. (*Lady in the Lake*, Raymond Chandler) (Buchanan, 1999, p.393)

Why did I choose this place, this airport? It was because of this very paradox, a place that is both strange and familiar. I was not particularly drawn to the aesthetics of such a place although I have become so. I was, instead, interested in document-ing these strange yet familiar spaces in which we spend ever increasing amounts of time; shopping malls, hotels, stations and airports. In this sense, the airport was an understandable choice. I had not anticipated the opinions that I am discussing here.

Non-Place

I have been questioning why I draw in-situ or in-place. Drawing these often barely inhabited corridors and spaces in the airport I have asked myself what it is about this process that I am drawn to or perhaps, more accurately, drawn in by. What happens when I draw in non-place, a place that is not concerned with identity and is measured in periods of time? The security conditions of the airport meant that I was not allowed to take photos for reference, as such my only way of recording the space was through drawing. This meant that all the drawings made for this research project were made in-situ and not retrospectively.

I have travelled through London Luton Airport many times and given little thought to the architecture or the sense of place. I get a vague feeling of being someone else in airports. This may be the constant barrage of instructions, both verbal and visual, meaning you make very few of your own decisions. Or the vast array of shopping experiences and often long stretches of time in which to indulge in them. But these are thoughts I have had recently, after the event. Indeed, when I went back to London Luton Airport for the first day of the residency, I was not sure that I had ever been there at all. Indeed, the drawings shown today could have been drawn in one of many airports across the UK, or indeed across the world.

Airports along with highways, hotels, and even cash machines can be defined as non-places. The very premise of these non-places relates to their standardisation as well as their lack of integration. Anthropologist Marc Augé coined the phrase 'non-place' in his essay and book of the same title, *Non-Places: Introduction to an Anthropology of Supermodernity* (1995). It is here that Augé gives an explanation of the relationship between space and non-space.

If a place can be defined as relational, historical and concerned with identity, then a space which cannot be defined as relational, or historical or concerned with identity will be a non-place (Augé, 1995, p.63).

Augé argues that these non-places do not integrate with those that have come before. Instead, they promote these existing places to the status of spectacle or 'places of memory'. He states that non-places are defined by their over-abundance of space and contain excessive information. The way we as travellers or visitors relate to non-places are through these instructions for use. The space of a non-place creates neither singular identity nor relations; only solitude and similitude. This definition of non-place provides a reason for the feelings I had when visiting the airport; had I ever been there?

Marc Augé states that non-places are a product of supermodernity. He defines supermodernity as an intensification of modernity and an emphasis on the ability of biology and technology to overcome all natural limitations. A profound lack of integration between past and present is caused by an outright repudiation of historical knowledge. The non-places of supermodernity are those that we feel we know even if we have not been there before. Augé tells us that airports are concerned with standardisation and are often remembered in very generic terms. One airport looks very much like the next. This provides an interesting dichotomy as the drawings produced here address a highly personal narrative; seen, imagined and remembered. In these drawings, space is distorted and stretched and perspectives are skewed. The expansive stretches of artificially tiled floors slope upwards and away from the bottom of the sketchbook. Non-spaces are measured in units of time. The time of check in and out or the time it takes to pass through define these places. Each is governed and experienced through itineraries, lengths of stay and timetables. It is the experience of these transient moments that is documented.

Encompassing Conversations

So far, I have attempted to understand the particulars of the place in which I was working. Now I will address what is happening between the subject and the paper when I draw in this non-place. There are numerous analogies for drawing that I could cite however I will refer to the English lexicon for clues. We say we are drawn to something or more specifically we are 'drawn into a conversation'. As if we are being physically pulled in. It is this being drawn to the subject that interests me and is what I believe is happening when I draw. Writer and art historian John Berger describes the intensity of looking and the energy of whatever is being scrutinised as being in discourse. The discourse he is commenting on is between the person drawing and the subject they are drawing from.

> The encounter of these two energies, their dialogue, does not have the form of question and answer. It is a ferocious and unarticulated dialogue (Berger, 2007, p.77).

I feel that Berger's suggestion that drawing is like a conversation is close to the way that I experience drawing. This is not a conversation with someone I know but with a stranger. Someone I am struggling to get to know, searching for common ground. I am trying to remember if I have met them before. This is the time in which objects shed their mute quality and speak (Trieb, 2008).

So drawing draws you in like pulling a thread, pulling it out of its knotted tangle (Taussig, 2011, p.xii). What of the time this process takes? I refer to Berger (2007) again who puts forward the notion that photography stops time whilst drawing encompasses it. When drawing there is a significant urge to stop time, to pause and return to the scene over and over again (Taussig, 2011, p.22). If you have ever drawn from life you will understand what I mean. However, this urge can be resisted (as I have attempted here) and the process of drawing is seen as the intended outcome. Drawings are left 'unfinished'. Where drawings are more prolonged they have as much to do with my recent memory of the scene as to that which was directly in front of me at that moment; that is if the conversation has been longer than a simple question and answer. I must be dredging my mind, searching for similar experiences on which to draw.

Memory and documentation co-exist in these images; the past and the present. I am as much documenting my own experiences and memories, as the subject in front of me. Johannes Fabian, cultural theorist and anthropologist, isolates these different forms of time. Fabian's seminal work *Time and the Other* (2002) advances the idea that these differing notions of time have caused a contradiction within the field of anthropology. In ethnographical fieldwork the anthropologist and the peoples being studied are contemporaries, existing in the same time and able to respond to one another and are in dialogue. On the other hand in anthropological writing, instead of acting as interlocutors, the people of the other culture become separate: an individual that the anthropologist observes or has observed form afar, or the 'Other'. Fabian calls this anthropology's 'denial of coevalness'; the denial that the anthropologist and the Other have existed in the same time and space. The former notion of time, is relevant to this discussion, Fabian calls this 'intersubjective' time (Fabian, 2005). Intersubjective time transpires in the interactions between two subjects in dialogue. It is associated with the way people relate both temporally and spatially. This is the notion of time in which these drawings take place. The drawings are both produced during and document intersubjective time.

Drawing the strands together

What I am trying to define here is personal and idiosyncratic. In the opening of this article, I stated that through the practice or act of drawing and being there I have explored the relationship between drawing and space. I was referring to being in the space and in front of whatever I was drawing. I meant quite literally that when I was drawing airport passengers, I was there in the departure lounge. This is obvious, of course, but what I have actually started to address is the notion of 'there' in less literal terms. I refer again to Berger (2007) who asks the question:

> Where are we, during the act of drawing, in spirit? Where are you at such moments – moments which add up to so many, one might think of them as another life-time? (Berger, 2007, p.123)

An answer could lie in understanding pictorial traditions:

> For instance, the European tradition, since the Renaissance, places the model over *there*, the draughtsman *here*, and the paper somewhere in between, within arms reach of the draughtsman, who observes the model and notes down what he has observed on the paper in front of him. (Berger, 2007, p.123 [authors emphasis])

Is there something in this – the opposition of here and there? Does the idea of being in a place (either here or there) have a significance to, or relationship with the act of drawing? Should I have called this article 'Being Here' as western drawing tradition dictates that is where we are when we draw; I am here and the thing I am drawing is over there. (Berger, 2007, p.123) This is a material understanding of the spatial relationship between draughtsman and what he is observing. But Berger quite clearly says 'in spirit', this does not denote a material stance. Therefore, is it through the drawing conversation that we pull ourselves closer to the subject? This may be the case but it does not help to make clear what has happened when drawing in a non-place. Berger was no doubt talking about drawings he made from the veranda of his Parisian home and not in the departure lounge of the Charles de Gaulle Airport.

Perhaps a temporal answer is needed rather than a spatial one (Berger, 2007) to fully understand the relationship between the process of drawing and non-place? Paul Klee's comment that the line 'goes out for a walk' (Klee, 1968, p.16), Klee's drawn line is ever changing; not fixed as an artifact might be, but constantly developing. A drawing is a process of continual corrections. A line is full of potential. It is in this sense a time-based medium. It is about becoming rather than being (Berger, 2007).

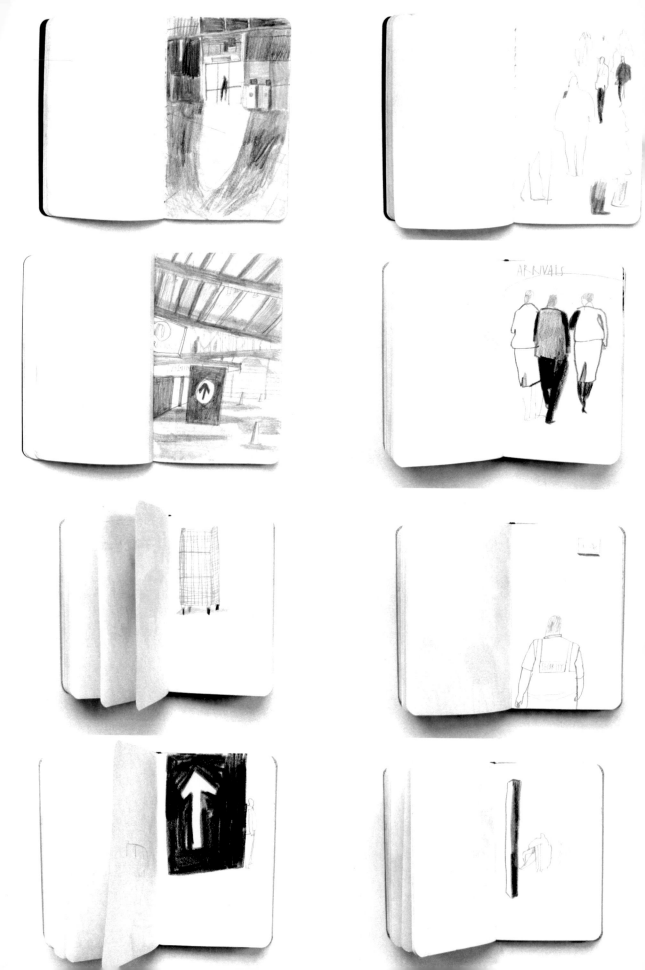

Augé states that non-places are there to be passed through and are therefore often measured in periods of time: timetables, departure times and itineraries. I have already discussed the inescapable urge to pause time when drawing and yet the obvious impossibility of doing so. Berger would have us believe that drawing encompasses time instead of stoppping it. These inherent qualities of drawing mean that the very essence of non-place is documented; the time in which it takes to pass through the space.

So drawings contain time. When writing about drawings in his fieldwork notebook, Taussig discusses the unique power of drawing as a visual document. He looks at the relationship drawing has with time slightly differently, suggesting:

The images that inhabit time – the recursive time of rereading – are historical, in a peculiar way. Being recursive, they flow with time yet also arrest it… They are allegories punched out of time waiting… Chronology is grasped and analyzed in a spatial image. (Taussig, 2011, p.53)

He is proposing that drawings explore and record the intersubjective time in which they were made. For Taussig, these drawings are documents; they are to be taken away from the scene and reread. What happens to these drawing of mine when they are taken away from the airport? Or indeed any documentary drawing when they are viewed after the event? If we look back to Fabian (2002) and the contradictions he sees in anthropological work, then the drawing as document can be seen as the 'anthropological writing'. Therefore separating, in this case, the draftsperson from the observed scene. Thus they are spatially and temporally different or representing the denial of coevalness as Fabian labels it. The denial is that the two have ever existed in the same time or space. Yet here is the very same contradiction that I am presenting you with. I have discussed at length the process of drawing whilst showing you the 'finished' drawing. However, (anthropological) writing and drawing are different acts. This is a relationship that has honoured much debate and discussion – though here it is enough to say that they are different. In the process of drawing, whether encompasses or grasping, time is made into a spatial image that lays bare the drawing activity. The resulting drawn document serves to lessen this denial of coevalness, by chronicling the inter-subjective time in which it was made.

This drawn document of the airport is unlike other forms of documentation. It not only contains time but also the empathetic nature of bearing witness. In these places of excess and individuality, these non-places, the strange and the familiar coexist through the very process of drawing.

Bibliography

Augé, M. (1995) *Non-places: introduction to the anthropology of supermodernity.* Verso, London.

Berger, J. (2007) *Berger on drawing.* Occasional Press, Aghabullogue, Cork.

Buchanan, I. (1999) *Non-places: space in the age of supermodernity,* Social Semiotics, vol. 9, no. 3, pp. 393-398.

Deleuze, G. & Guattari, F. (2004) *A thousand plateaus capitalism and schizophrenia.* Continuum, London.

Fabian, J. (2002) *Time and the other: how anthropology makes its object.* Columbia University Press, New York.

Garner, S.W. (2008) *Writing on drawing: essays on drawing practice and research.* Intellect, Bristol.

Ingold, T. (2013) *Making: anthropology, archaeology, art and architecture.* Routledge, Farnham.

Klee, P. (1968) *Pedagogical sketchbook.* Faber & Faber, London.

Taussig, M. (2011) *I swear I saw this: drawings in fieldwork notebooks, namely my own.* University Of Chicago Press, London.

Treib, M. (2008) *Drawing/thinking: confronting an electronic age.* Routledge, Oxon.

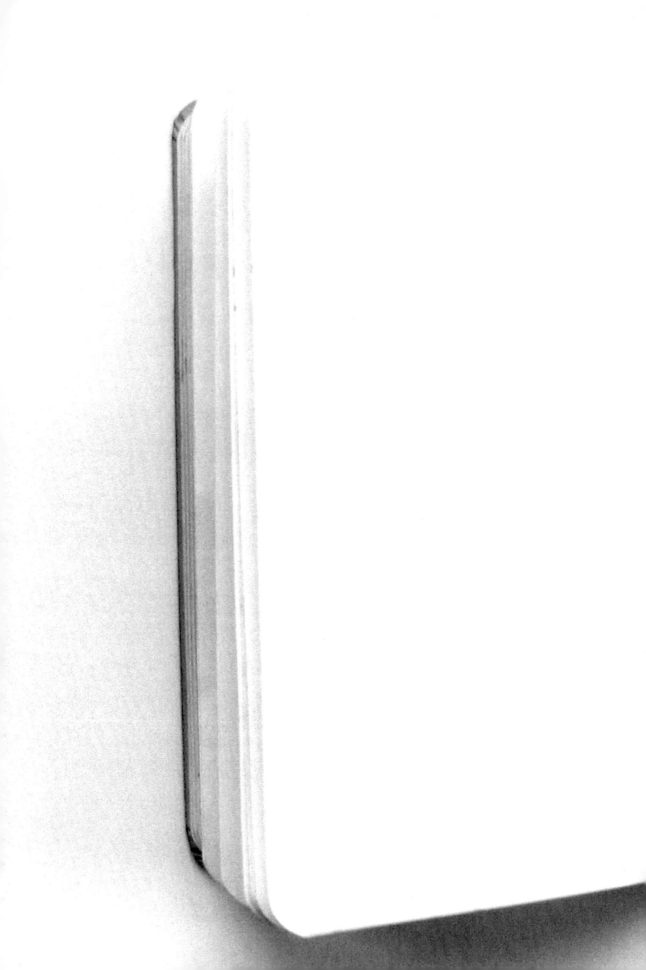

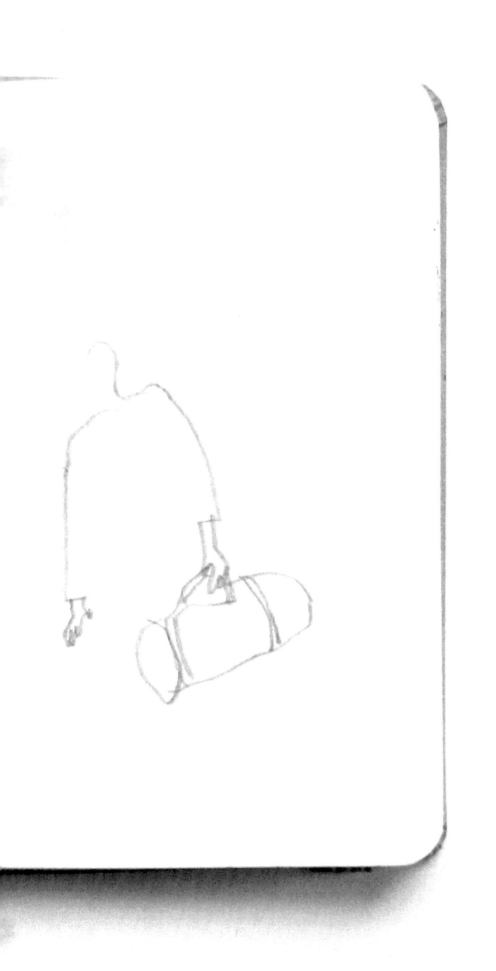

BEHIND THE SCENES OF CONTEMPORARY CHILEAN CINEMA

María-Paz Peirano

The tenth Glasgow Film Festival opens this February, and is giving particular attention to its CineChile sidebar, which.promises to reflect the breadth and diversity of innovative new films emerging from the southern tip of the Americas. Chilean critic and film scholar Maria Paz-Peirano explores the roots of this new flowering, and the sort of new work we can expect to see at GFF 2014.

CANANA
presenta

SELECCIÓN OFICIAL DE CHILE AL OSCAR®

GAEL
GARCÍA BERNAL

NO

LA CAMPAÑA QUE CAMBIÓ A UNA NACIÓN

CANNES
QUINCENA DE REALIZADORES
GANADOR

SAN SEBASTIÁN
HORIZONTES LATINOS

LOCARNO
INT'L FILM FESTIVAL

TORONTO
INT'L FILM FESTIVAL

TELLURIDE
INT'L FILM FESTIVAL

NEW YORK
INT'L FILM FESTIVAL

NOVIEMBRE 2012

 CANANA   XX DOS EQUIS   GRUPOHABITA   @CANANApresenta   #NoLaPelícula   /CANANApresenta

On January 2013, the film *No (Larraín 2012)* was nominated to the Oscar for Best Foreign Language film. It was the first time a Chilean film had ever run for the Academy awards. A month later, *Gloria (Lelio 2012)* became the first Chilean film in ten years to participate in the Official competition of the Berlinale, where it won the Best Actress award. These achievements led to both films enjoying wide acclaim in the international world of cinema. Chilean cinema thus accomplished two major historical achievements in a short period of time, something that had rarely been experienced before by this small, peripheral cinematography.

Clearly, the conjunction of these events is not a coincidence. Chilean cinema has flourished in the international context over the past few years. Film production, along with its global circulation and exhibition, has expanded considerably, and the international media has been describing this phenomenon as a possible new "boom" for peripheral cinemas, as was the case for other 'world' cinematographies before, such as those of Argentina or Iran. Whether this will also be the case for Chilean cinema is yet to be seen, although, in truth, Chilean film now exists in the international sphere like never before. Chilean films have been increasingly selected to participate in all major films festivals of the world, such as Cannes, Berlin, Venezia, San Sebastián and Sundance, as well as being part of the film selection in several of the most prestigious of the smaller film festivals. Some of these events have been programming special focuses on Chilean cinema, and films such as *Bonsai* (Jiménez 2011), *Summer* ('Verano', Torres Leiva 2011) *Dog's Flesh* ('Carne de Perro', Guzzoni 2012), *From Thursday till Sunday* ('De Jueves a Domingo', Sotomayor 2012), *Things the way they are* ('Las Cosas Como Son', Lavanderos 2012), *Young and wild* ('Joven y Alocada', Rivas 2012), *The Illiterates* ('Las Analfabetas', Moisés Sepúlveda 2013) and *The Quispe girls* ('Las Niñas Quispe', Sebastián Sepúlveda 2013), just to name a few, have been successfully circulating throughout the international circuit the last couple of years.

These films have usually received positive critical reception, also winning various awards, particularly in the slots for young independent directors. For instance, Fernando Guzzoni's *Dog's Flesh* won the New Directors section of San Sebastián in 2012. In the same year, Dominga Sotomayor's *From Thursday till Sunday* won the Tiger Award in Rotterdam, while Fernando Lavanderos *'Things the way they are'* secured the Forum of independents award in Karlovy-Vary in 2013. Moreover, a good number of Chilean films have received international funding in later years, winning some of the "work in progress" prizes before their release, as was the case with Gloria, which secured the *Cine en Construcción* ('*Films in Progress*') award in San Sebastián in 2012.

How could this recent upsurge of Chilean Cinema be explained? Apart from the distinctive quality one could identify in the films of the so-called *Novísimo Cine Chileno* ('Newest' Chilean cinema), one could also look for additional answers in the recent developments of the context in which Chilean cinema is produced. The conditions have changed in such a way that they have facilitated, and led to an increase in, the production of movies. The new context has also made increasingly visible this small cinematography at an international level. This shift in the production – and by extension, circulation and exhibition – of Chilean films has been the result of the articulation of both national and international trends.

To begin with, international film festivals have played a major role in the production and circulation of Chilean cinema, as had happened with other peripheral cinemas. Those 'world' small film industries made in the margins of the dominant (that is to say, Hollywood-like) modes of production and distribution, find in the international film festivals a relatively stable channel of exhibition. Festivals enable the circulation of certain types of non-mainstream cinematographic works, so to a certain extent, they collaborate to expand small internal film markets. At the same time, they participate in the add-value process of the films, which gain prestige with their circulation; and they also help to support local production. Indeed, Chilean film has been promoted not only through direct funding provided by some festivals (like the Hurbert Bals Fund of Rotterdam Film Festival, for independent world cinema), but also through the possibility to establish economic exchanges and agreements inside the markets, co-production forums and other 'industry' spaces hosted by the festivals.

While this new international context of production and distribution is certainly important, the presence of Chilean cinema in the global film scene can only be fully understood if we also look into its historical local transformations. The specificities of Chilean contemporary film industry are undoubtedly framed in the post-dictatorship economic and political context. The change to a democratic system in the early nineties implied a significant transformation in the context of production, including the legal framework of the audio-visual production, the funding system and the possibilities of exhibition. While with the new status of Chile as a democratic country implied a decrease in international funding to Chilean filmmakers – that had aimed to ease its authoritarian, 'third world' condition, the state would eventually serve as a major sponsor for the local industry. The beginning of the 1990s saw a modification in the institutional frame that would allow for the development of Chilean film industry, in comparison to previous years, when Chilean film production had practically disappeared.

Since the flourishing moment of the New Latin-American cinema in the late 1960s, and its brief position as a "revolutionary art" sponsored by Allende's socialist government (1970–1973), Chilean cinema had suffered an important downturn since the Military coup (1973). Almost every film director had to escape abroad, and they were dedicated to making films whose main themes were related to the Coup, the dictatorship and political exile. Meanwhile, during the military government only a few productions were made and exhibited in Chile itself. The state had legally abandoned any support to local cinema, by means of decree n.825 (1974) that set Chilean Cinema under the regulations of a free market. Audio-visual producers sprouted from advertising, and concomitantly filmed militant documentary films. More expensive feature films had alternative funding from private companies or international institutions like Human Rights NGOs.

The post-dictatorship Concertación government (a centre-left coalition in power from 1990 to 2010) then designed a political programme that intended to recover the cultural policies the dictatorship had suspended. For that reason, it created the Department of Audio-visual and Cinema at the Ministry of Education in order to design programs to support the film industry. In addition, it introduced the Fund for Arts and Culture (FONDART), which provided public funding for the sector; and in 1999 CORFO (Corporation for the Promotion of Production) also set a special programme for the promotion of the audio-visual industry, which co-financed both the development of film projects and their national and international distribution. These policy changes made a significant impact on the production of films, which by the 2000s was largely funded by the Chilean state, besides a secondary contribution from private companies and international co-production agreements.[1] Furthermore, after a long political struggle, the "Law of Cinema" was finally promulgated in 2004, which set a specific fund dedicated for the audio-visual sector. This fund also aimed to grant financial aid for the diffusion of audio-visual projects, via the participation in international film festivals and markets, among other forms of support.

As a result, during the period between 1990 and 2013 there was a significant rise in annual Chilean film production. The numbers are, of course, even larger after the changes policy since the mid-2000s, which also concurred with the emerging international funding possibilities mentioned above. Furthermore, this new scenario coincided with other elements that have had an impact on the expansion of national production, like the decrease of the costs of production and the emergence of local film schools. Firstly, the technological change in the last decade had a great impact on the production expenses, which were reduced thanks to the appearance of the HDV (digital format) in 2005. At the same time, the number of Chilean film professionals has increased, related to the several private film schools created since the mid-nineties, after the closure of the university film schools during the military government. The latter has also contributed to the emergence of a number of specialized professionals including filmmakers, producers and film scholars who have all played a part in the constitution of a new field of local film production.

1   For example, between 1990 and 1998, eleven feature films were released through funding from FONDART, which amounts to 39% of the total production. Between 1999 and 2002, of the 46 films premiered in that period (both feature and documentary films), 90% of funds were from the state. Source: Chilean Council of Audiovisual Art and Industry at www.consejodelacultura.cl/chileaudiovisual

Interestingly enough, this post-dictatorship expansion of the field is not isolated from the economic system imposed during the military regime. Since Pinochet's dictatorship, Chile has had a free market economy based on deeply neo-liberal policies, where the government's role in the economy is mostly limited to (usually loose) regulation. This has resulted in a quite steady increase of domestic and foreign private investment. Chilean Economy was, throughout the nineties and 2000s, growing at impressive rates (GDP averaged around 8%), which led to the way the country is now perceived – internally and internationally – as a model for economic success. This image of success derived from the outstanding macro-economic indicators contrast, however, with the country's high levels of social inequality,[2] which have led to an explosion of social movements demanding deep, structural changes since 2010. In this context, the support given to the audio-visual sector still does not cover deeper changes in the regulations on film production, distribution and exhibition, and the industry remains fairly unprotected. Moreover, while later Chilean governments have indeed attempted to restore the role of state in the promotion of arts and culture, their policies also seek to reinforce the state's main project of constituting Chilean cinema as an economically successful national industry, following a neo-liberal model. Thus, the relationship between Chilean cinema and the state is mainly one where the latter subsidises private investors (producers) who are expected to enhance the industry and brand a 'national image', collaborating to position national products abroad. The financial support for the participation of Chilean film professionals in international film markets and festivals can be understood as part of this project.

The concurrence of these production conditions have had an impact not only in the number but also in the type of films made in this context. Chilean cinema has never been as diverse as today. The films that are part of this 'boost' address themes that had been largely absent from Chilean cinematography, mainly because the new conditions allow those multiple possibilities. The new generation of filmmakers has been seeking for the renovation of Chilean film, moving away from the predominant (though fragmented) Chilean cinematographic tradition.

Chilean cinema, influenced by the New Latin-American cinema movement of the 1960s, has historically attributed a central position to the socio-political content of films. Even during the late nineties, when most feature films did not have a clear political aspiration, Chilean cinema seemed attached to a certain social responsibility to show or "represent" the local. Films tended to reconstruct images that were mainly based on Chilean popular culture and usually in reference to urban slums or popular low-class characters. By contrast, later Chilean cinema has generally avoided those more typical paths, without making more explicit socio-political discourses on the dictatorship, inequality, and violence; that is to say, the contradictions of Chilean neo-liberal society.

There is certain 'cosmopolitan' look in the Chilean films circulating nowadays in the international market, which differs from more locally based aesthetics. I would say that the training received at film schools, plus the intensified participation of Chilean filmmakers in the international sphere since mid-2000s, has also resulted in the introduction and spread of new aesthetics and narratives forms. The 'Newest' Chilean films tend to narrate intimate, small stories. They normally have a slow rhythm, and they are composed of contemplative and beautifully framed shots. These new aesthetic forms are clearly consistent with the international trends in contemporary independent filmmaking.

As might be expected, this type of Chilean film has encountered varied criticism in Chile, where film scholars and critics have been pointing out the apparent lack of socio-political commitment of this type of cinema. Actually, from that perspective, both the themes and the sophisticated aesthetics of this 'Newest' Chilean cinema could be interpreted as 'self-absorbed' and elitist. The films have thus been deemed to be a reflection of the triumph of the neo-liberal system in Chilean culture. However, while in fact we could identify certain disengagement between some films and Chilean society (and audiences), I would say that the diversity and subtleness of recent Chilean cinema tends to be overlooked in these discourses and interpretations.

2　Source: Organisation for Economic Co-operation and Development (OECD) www.oecd.org

Contemplation on present-day solitude, the elabora-tions over the aim for success, and the fragmenta-tion of everyday social experience, are actually all common themes explored by the 'Newest' Chilean cinema, and certainly those are not just unreflective symptoms of contemporary Chilean society. Actually, they could be read as critical observations on the broader context. Furthermore, direct social commen-tary is not absent from some of the more successful local productions. The references to the Chilean political past are still there: Dog's Flesh, which is about a former torturer of Pinochet's regime; or the film No, documenting the advertising campaign that facilitated winning the Chilean referendum in 1988 that ended with the 16-year military dictatorship. Clearly, this film does not really consider the total complexity of that historical moment, but refers to a small story in that context, reflecting at the same time on the current conditions of the Chilean politi-cal and economic system. On the other hand, some of the present-day social and political struggles are indirectly tackled in many other films. Gloria, for instance, is focused on the life, frustrations and dreams of a mature woman in that particular local context. Despite the fact that the story is quite 'uni-versal', the film includes some small comments and images about recent Chilean social movements and students' protests, even when those remarks could remain unnoticed for foreign audiences

The recent flourishing of Chilean cinema, as the type of films circulating nowadays in the international film circuit, definitively registers its production conditions and the broader social, political and economic context in which they are made. 'Newest' Chilean cinema could be interpreted as a result, as a symptom, or as a reflective response on the local and international context, regarding larger issues in the political economy of Chilean society, as well as the production conditions of contemporary peripheral cinemas. Hopefully, this boost that facilitates the access of worldwide audiences to these films, will foster curiosity over some non-mainstream film productions, and so opening up the familiarisation, at the same time, with the societies where they are made.

24

Raymond Burke

CLOSE

Flat 24

Naw. Yer no' gettin' another biscuit. Ye've left a hauf eaten wan on the erm o' the couch. Eat that wan... Naw don't eat that wan. It's boggin. Geezit. I'll pit it in the bin. What a waste. Jist stay there fur a minute. Try no' tae fa' aff the couch.

Here. Be careful wi' that wan, noo. I'll be glad when you go tae the school. Sittin' aboot here all day tidying up efter ye.

Bloody dug. Listen to it. Whit a racket. There should be a law against that. Breach of the peace. Waking people up. Maybe get you a dug when your aulder. Wid ye like that? No' a big dug. Jist a wee wan. A nice wee staffie or something. A wee dug tae look efter us. Wid get us oot the hoose a bit merr, tae. Maybe go up the centre in yer pram later. Eh? As long as we don't see his mither. Tryin' tae make me feel guilty. Fur nuthin'. But at least we'll get a wee walk. Get a bit o' fresh air. Anyway, shut up the noo. Ah'm watching this.

Well, that's another 'oor ah'll never get back. Ye hungry?

Ah should huv registered you wi' that nursery when I hud the chance. Too much of a walk, though. Every day up and doon that hill. And huvin' tae talk to all thae other mothers. Talking pish. Wantin' tae know aw yer business. The school's much nearer anyway. We'll jist wait for that. Only a couple o' years. We'll be well oot o' here in oor ain place by then. Ah don't know how the cooncil have to put us in emergency accom first. How can they no' jist stick us straight intae a new hoose? Ah suppose when we get a new hoose – might be miles away – we can sort you out wi' a nursery or school then. Nae panic the noo. Then ah'll get back tae work. Wull ye miss yer mammy? Aye ye wull. Anyway, when ah've got a job... or maybe ah'll go tae Uni... then if I get a really good job, ah'll pay somebody else tae look efter ye. Naw, ah widny dae that. Takes a couple o' years anyway, ah think.

Yer da will be back oot by then. Should'a hung the bastard. Whit he did tae me. Majin that? Man hittin' a wummin? Wisny the first time either. Done it before anaw. Fuckin' polis didny dae nuthin' aboot it jist cause ah widny press charges. Third time he made the mistake o' daein' it in public. Hope you don't turn oot like him. Ah'll make sure ye don't. You'll be clever and learn tae respect women. Know what he said to me on only oor second date? "If ye want tae go oot wi' me, ye don't talk tae other men." Aw ah did wis huv a wee chat to the taxi driver. Jist huving a laugh. But he wis ragin'. Ripped the shoulder of my new dress, tae.

Still. He apologised. Said it was jist his way of showin' how much he liked me. Angie telt me tae dump him, but she never really knew him right. He always apologised. Bought me flowers an' that. Sometimes chocolates but he didny want me to lose my figure. Cheeky bastard but he always apologised. Ah think Angie fancied him a wee bit. Good looking man. Just like yersel. Who's ma handsome wee man? Eh? Who's ma handsome wee man?

Look at the mess. Ye've got crumbs everywhere. Calm down Ah'm just wiping the chocolate aff yer face. There you are. Relax. Ah'll pit the telly oan again.

Ah know it's the ice cream van. Wull ye shut it? Just cos a bell rings doesny mean ye've got tae get sweeties. Anyway, whit's the point in an ice cream van when the shops are open? Doesn'y even gie tic... according to her up in nummer twenty six. Weird thing to say oot o' the blue. Why wid she say that? Don't think she's short o' a bob or two. Sits on her arse aw day while her man's oot graftin' aw night.

Where ur ye gaun noo? Stoap playing wi' thae curtains. Mind we're oan the grun flerr. Don't want people knowing oor business. Ah said don't open them! The light shines aff the telly. I could maybe go oan wan o' these quiz shows. Make masel a couple of grand. Dead easy. Whit city is it? Em... Ah know this wan... Paris! Bang on! See, son? Yer maw's no' that daft.

Ah wis always good at geography. Even better at maths. Ye didny know that did ye? Ah worked in the bookies afore you popped oot on the scene. The computer did all the calculations and that, but I could've worked it oot masel if ah hud tae. Ah could've. Good job that. Ah could maybe go back.

1963? Clinton.

Kennedy? How the fuck is emdy supposed tae know that? Pish.

Dae ye want a wee cartoon, son? Here... ah'll stick ye back on the chair. Aw right, then. Lie on the flerr if ye like.

Ah'm jist gaun fur a coffee. Do you want a drink fae the fridge? Orange? Oh, purple wan? Geeza minute.

There ye go.

Ah wonder if he knows wherr we urr? Naw. We'd have hud a letter of apology by noo. Ah know him, he canny know. But he'll find oot eventually. Better no' come roon here or wherever we end up. They said ah can get a restraining order if ah ask. Angie says ah'll end up taking him back. Whit's she like? First she wants me to dump him and then she says ah'll take him back. No way. No danger, wee man. We can look efter oorselves.

There's the buzzer gaun up the sterr somewhere.

Oh, look at the mess yer making. That'll stain that carpet. Jist geezit. Ah'll get a cloth. Don't start greetin'. It's awright. Ye can have another drink. Jist wait till ah've cleared up this wan. Okay, darling?

Fuck. Whit noo? Calm doon. It's jist the buzzer. Stay wherr ye urr. Ah'll get it. Wonder who that is? Here's me wi' ma dressin' goon oan. Whit time is it? Fuck.

Er... Hello? Thirty two? Naw... this is twenty four. Aye. Maybe he's switched it aff right enough. Aye. Nae bother, pal. In ye come.

METAMORPHO-RISS

Johnny Rodger

Egon Riss:
a Golden Ass-been?
(with thanks to JAF MacDonald)

The Metamorphoses of Apuleius, which St. Augustine referred to as *The Golden Ass* (Asinus aureus), is the only ancient novel in Latin to survive in its entirety. The protagonist of the novel is called Lucius. The plot revolves around the protagonist's curiosity *(curiositas) and insatiable desire to see and practice magic. While trying to perform a spell to transform into* a bird, he is accidentally transformed into an ass. This leads to a long journey, literal and metaphorical, filled with in-set tales. He finally finds salvation through the intervention of the goddess Isis, whose cult he joins. (wikipaedia last viewed 22/11/13)

The name Egon Riss is not one which is generally taken to resound through the Scottish Halls of Fame and Renown. It would, indeed, astonish many people to hear it mentioned alongside the name of a fellow Jewish refugee from the Nazi-dominated German lands, Isi Metzstein, as of significance in the pantheon of makers of post-war Scottish modern architecture. The relative silence is nevertheless understandable: not only does his output not 'survive in its entirety', but there is almost no evidence of major structures ever designed and built by Riss in current day Scotland. Yet Egon Riss was as echt a creator of the mid-twentieth century Scottish built environment as GKC, Robert Matthews, Basil Spence or Peter Wormersley. At his peak in the sixties over ten thousand people occupied and used his buildings on a daily basis, and more concrete was probably poured under his design and direction than under anyone else's at that period.

So who was Egon Riss, what did he make, how substantial and significant was it, and what evidence of it, physical or otherwise, remains to this day?

Riss (1901–64) was born in a part of the Austro-Hungarian province of Galicia which is now Southern Poland. Educated in Vienna and at the Weimar Bauhaus, he knew Kokoschka and Klee, and had already built various hospital buildings, structures in the Silesian coalfields, and a café in the Wiener Werkbund before he fled the Nazis in 1938, originally to Czechoslovakia, and subsequently to England. On arrival in England he was given much support by the architectural profession: the RIBA intervened to secure his release from internment, and the Architects' Czechoslovakian Refuge Fund paid for his accommodation in London. Posterity has not quite seen fit to be so generous with Riss as were his fellow professionals in his alien land of refuge though. As we shall see below, his only complete, unaltered and original designed structure which remains in this country is somewhat egregious in character. For despite his extensive output, his built work was a prime victim of both the post-modernist purges of concrete, and of the collapse of industrial production and infrastructure in the late 20th century.

While some modernist architects attempted to make an exclusivist virtue out of disappointment and evident design failure in the disappearance of one's creative output (for example, Metzstein formed a 'virtual' institution, the Macallan Club whose entrance requirements were that one of your buildings had been demolished in your lifetime), Riss could be said to have suffered more ignominiously than most. Oddly and unfortunately, it was in those early days of his arrival in these islands that Riss undertook the one commission that was to constitute his lasting design legacy here. Just a few years before his arrival, Penguin books had (in 1935) started to produce their then innovative new design of paperback books. These books were handy, lightweight, modern and accessible. Riss was commissioned by the design company Isokon to come up with a smallish piece of furniture which could sit nearby an armchair and stack numbers of those small books within easy arm's reach. The final design – of which only 100 were produced in 1939 before war broke out – was an unusual shaped bent birch ply magazine /book rack which has an Eames-like profile, and can carry magazines and newspapers as well as the paper-backs in various formats. It is now a prized collectors' piece despite the clumsy zoological hybrid-sounding name –the 'Penguin Donkey'. Indeed before extolling the beauty of the object itself, one commentator says of that name – 'it sounds like a particularly nauseating carnival exhibit'.

It is, thus, not too much of an asinine stretch to say that, like Lucius, the protagonist in 2nd Century AD Roman writer Apuleius' novel 'Metamorphosis', Riss finds himself trapped posthumously, as it were, in the body of a Donkey. Again, just like Lucius, Riss conjured up his 'Golden Ass' himself. But where Lucius' Ass is a literary construct, a metaphor for the stumbling oafishness of his unthinking curiosity which imprisons him for eight out of the eleven chapters of that book, Riss's Donkey is an all too solid and real – if bizarrely unrepresentative – remnant of his creative life, and embodiment of his reputation. Yet perhaps, as in the case of Apuleius and his character Lucius, the only way to free Riss from the little barrel-body of the donkey is through words, by telling his story and reworking it with images and the fuller details of his creative life.

Riss served in the Royal Engineers during the War, and not long after (1947) he gained appointment as the Chief Production Architect at the Scottish Division of the National Coal Board. He stayed in that position until his death in 1964.With the nationalisation of the coal mining industry after the War, there was a massive reorganisation and rationalisation of the organisation of employees, sites and production. Previously there had been hundreds of small pits in private ownership dotted around the various coalfields in the country. Many of these mines were unproductive, had poor working and safety conditions, and poor facilities, in terms of baths, changing rooms etc for the workers. Not only was the new National Coal Board formed and swept along with the great social and collective enthusiasm at large in the country after the War, but there was specifically a great bouyancy in the industry, with optimistic consumption predictions for the era of rebuilding, and a vast programme of reconstruction. Hundreds of the small mines were shut down and small numbers of massive new colleries were built, which mined deeper down than ever before, and employed thousands of men on each site. These vast new pit complexes dominated landscapes with tall sleek modernist concrete structures symbolising optimism for the future, efficiency, and mastery of the world and its resources.

Riss himself was responsible for the design and construction of five of these superpits as well as various extensions and ancillary buildings designed on other sites. It is when we see his drawings and photos of these vast modernist complexes : at Bilston Glen, Lothian (completed 1952), Rothes, Fife (1957), Killoch, Ayrshire (1959), Monktonhall, Lothian (1965) and Seafield, Fife (1965): that we find it hard to believe that all that exists of this man's original, unaltered output is a wooden donkey of diminutive domestic scale.

These pits all have that similar heroic modernist look to them with the tall concrete slabs housing the winding gear, and there is undoubtedly, from the photographs at any rate, a poetic and existential evocation in volume, balance and clean engineered lines, of man's industrial engagement with the land. Yet despite the sculptural hymning to collective endeavour we see in the physical forms there, and the attempt in those clean international modernist forms to move beyond historicism, each pit has a specific and individual history to tell. Each of those industrial sites has also now disappeared: demolished in the wake of the collapse of the industry in the 1980s.

Of those individual stories, the Rothes Colliery in Fife is the shortest, and was perhaps the most immediately disappointing as it was the only one which shut down in Riss's lifetime. Opened in 1958, with the New Town of Glenrothes being built alongside it to house the workers, it was expected to cost £1.65M, to have a lifespan of 100 years, and for 1200 workers to produce 5000 tons of coal per day. In the end however, the pit cost £20M,and unexpected geological problems and flooding led to very poor productivity and its closure after only five years. Wider social repercussions of the failure included the redesignating of Glenrothes New Town as a centre for overspill population from Glasgow, rather than as a town for local mineworkers. The two concrete winding towers were demolished in 1993.

Of the two Riss designed superpits which were completed after his death, Monktonhall, opened 1967 (the other was Seafield opened 1965) was the deepest mine in the country, with two shafts sunk to over 900m depth. Buildings included workshops, admin buildings, baths, canteens and medical facilities for over 1600 workers. In the NCB era it had the assured market of the coal fired power station in nearby Cockenzie, but nonetheless it was shut down, or rather mothballed in the wake of the

'84 Miners' Strike and the McGregor rationalisation of the industry in 1987. The history did not end there however. Several groups of miners from the different coalfields – Ayrshire, Fife and Lothian – got together, and pooled their own savings (£10k per worker) to buy the pit and re-open it in 1992 as Britain's largest private mine. It was now the only deep coal mine in Scotland. The story of the collective enterprise, their struggle to reopen the coalface, and work coal commercially, is recounted in the series of candid engagements represented in David Peat's STV documentary 'This Mine is Ours' (1994). The film follows the miners as they work to open up a new seam of coal, and get their first commercial contracts, before running into financial difficulties one year later. The precise nature of these difficulties are not specified in the film, although it ends suddenly with what appears to be an ominous change of staffing in the administration of the mine. As events turned out, a commercial concern Waverley Mining Finance stepped into the fray at that moment, and thenceforth took an ever increasing role in the running of the mine. Waverley eventually shut the whole operation down again in 1997. The first of Riss's concrete towers there was demolished that year, and the second followed a year later. It is said that some of the miners made up to thirty times their original investment at the time of the closure.

Thus, just as the story of Scotland's superpits can be characterised as a three decade descent from hero to zero, then simultaneously it seems, does the reputation of Riss shrink from that of a demiurge who conceived and engineered the large scale environmental aesthetic for a modern industry to a mere dabbler in dinky interior design. But perhaps the best epitaph for the dematerialised industry, and one which, paradoxically, could physically rescue Riss from the footnotes of zoomorphic design triviality and put his career once more in the profound, authentic and humane light it indisputably deserves, were his own words on that industry:

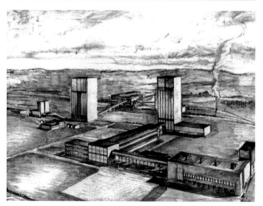

Mining is risky and powerful… it has its own very powerful rhythm, its own monumentality and its own frustration and despair. Mining is more than just a modern industry. It is a deep human experience which must also find its artistic expression in its own architecture.

We could debate about the 'rhythm' and the 'monumentality' of individual pieces of furniture, and there is no doubt that 'expression' is at a premium in interior design. It seems reasonable, nonetheless, to assert Riss's the last sentence there, is, after all, not the sort of thing which you would say about a one-off bookcase called 'donkey'.

ELECTRIC PASTORALE

Frances Robertson

Figure 1: Photograph from *The Galloway Hydro-Electric Development* (1938): Tongland Sluice gates

Visions of pastoral arcadias are a sure-fire provocation to every right thinking cultural critic; metropolitan literati and art historians are only too ready to unmask the 'dark side of the landscape', or the bourgeois rapacity of 'agrarian capitalism' to anyone foolish enough to admire a pleasant green expanse of woods, fields and waters (Barrell 1980; Williams 1975).

In this debate, 'pastoral' has a specific connotation, referring not simply to the poetic genre inherited from the classical and Renaissance worlds—in which country virtue is opposed to city vice—but instead to the re-working and re-appropriation of these ideas in late eighteenth century elite culture, with particular reference to the construction of the landed estate and its neo-classical representation both in paintings and in ambitious landscaping projects in the 'Capability Brown' mode. Such critiques of this area of enlightenment culture are old news now. In today's heritage industries our knowledge that Austen's heroines and their gracious country piles were in fact nurtured on city jobbery or the blood of plantation slaves no longer comes as some kind of horrible revelation, but instead adds a kind of burnished glow, a significant extra layering of the visitor experience. Even though we know these sub-texts, many city dwellers still harbour a kind of baffled rural nostalgia, a nest of concepts about place, nation, and identity that are far too complex to be laughed off as mere false consciousness.

In Scotland, we see such nostalgia expressed most obviously in the cult of the romantic Highlands that became as precious to the hard-bitten urban proletariat of red Clydeside as it was to tourists, landlords, and hoteliers in the tartan heartlands (Harvie 1977; Gold and Gold 1995). Indeed,

and despite the fact that the Clearances, forced emigration, and other 'improvements' were such recent events in popular memory, the compensating myth of an ancient, unspoilt northern wilderness was so strong that in the period before the Second World War many Scottish working class socialists formed an unlikely alliance with conservative lairds in strident opposition to various hydro scheme proposals in the Highlands – because they were seen as intrusions into nature (Payne 1988). Loyalty to that rugged style of artificial northern wilderness is perhaps one reason why other equally intrusive hydro-electric power schemes south of the Highland line did go ahead without controversy in 1930s Scotland, in the Clyde Valley and in Galloway, even though they were also located in rural areas of great natural beauty. Galloway is now perceived as a backwater of forests, lakes, second homes, communes and other retreats from contemporary life; its natural resources, even its primordially dark night sky, are now heavily protected. In striking contrast to these current perceptions of landscape amenity and its need for protection we will see that the pre-War hydro-electric power stations and dams in Galloway were presented as stark and confident expressions of modernist engineered prowess, making no attempt to nestle under a camouflage of nature, or the mantle of traditional building languages (as was the case with later post-War NOSHEB schemes in the Highlands; Glendinning 1997). This article will examine the interaction of landscape aesthetics, ideas of cultural and national identity, and notions of progressive modernism in the Galloway hydro schemes of the 1930s. We see a form of modernity derived not simply from the growth of cities, but nurtured by earlier, more agrarian projects of national improvement that also supported the pastoral myths floated in the Georgian era.

As every washed-out camper knows, Galloway is a beautiful green area of Lowland Scotland blessed with heavy and constant rainfall. Until around 1750, it had been an isolated, somewhat threatening area to outsiders (and indeed, natives too) with an economy not unlike that of the Scottish Highlands, of cattle keeping, trading and thieving, and home weaving of wool and linen textiles. But in the hundred years between 1750 and 1850, local landowners, entrepreneurs and external investors engaged in many modernising initiatives to encourage local industries, and this expanding economic development led to an increased population engaged in many new manufacturing occupations in textile mills and in other early industrial/ agrarian activities such as brewing or leatherworking. At this date, before railways, Galloway conducted its trade by sea as did most other parts of Britain, and it was therefore as

Figure 2: Photograph from *The Galloway Hydro-Electric Development* (1938)

'connected', as busy and successful in its economy, as other areas such as the north of England or Central Scotland that would later come to eclipse this region with the scale of their continued industrial expansion (Donnachie 1971). While the landed gentry were improving their estates through enclosures, parks and experimental farming practices to create new and fashionable 'pastoral' landscapes, other equally bold interventions into the landscape were in hand between these private domains. These included water powered textile mills, harbour construction, and, after the establishment of the Turnpike Trusts in 1780, strategic, engineered roads (Donnachie 1971: 26–7). Bridges marked intersections in these networks of communication and production; the bridge crossing the River Dee crossing at Tongland (constructed 1803–5) was styled in a deliberately rustic Picturesque manner by Thomas Telford in collaboration with the landscape artist Alexander Nasmyth (Ruddock 2000: 134), and embellished with chunky pointed gothick arches above the pedestrian towpaths on either side of the main river span. Its historical references were not intended to make this bridge look old, but were consciously designed as a bold monument of contemporary design. Around 1800 Galloway was as 'modern' as anywhere else outside in Britain. Moreover, the forces of modernisation at work were not really hidden by the classicising landscaping

efforts of the landed gentry because enclosure and 'improvement' were current topics of public attention, debate, and conflict.

By mid-century however, Galloway's economy did start to fall into decline, and in a couple of generations by 1900 the region had already taken on the quaint aspect of a rural backwater. Galloway's economic depression was in reality only one localised symptom of a more widespread underlying Scottish economic malaise that was caused, in the words of the infuriated George Malcolm Thomson, by the fact that the nation had become merely 'an annexe, half-industrial, half-sporting, of English civilisation' (from *Caledonia, or the Future of the Scots* 1926, quoted in Harvie 1977: 113). In 1900 however, such economic woes were not yet obvious in commercial cities such as Glasgow. To many entrepreneurial, art-loving middle class bohemians of urban Scotland, Galloway now appeared as a fine bolt-hole, and easily accessible by new transport connections. *Fin de siecle* artists such as E.A. Hornel and Jessie M. King with houses in Kirkudbright encouraged the formation of an artist's colony in the town, and their hedonistic and aesthetic approaches to art contributed to a colouristic version of modernism that underscored the pastoral image of this area. Indeed, a form of pastoral landscape representation continued to hold sway more generally in radical

Scottish art at the start of the twentieth century for despite artists' familiarity with avant garde European movements, much of their work, according to Tom Normand, remained fairly conservative, decorative and with a view that painting should be a celebration of nature and the natural (Normand 2003: 3). Nevertheless some artists such as William McCance resisted and mocked these tendencies, whether they appeared in the loathed couthiness of the kailyard artists or in the aesthetic explorations of more advanced art. McCance's early works were heavily influenced by the style and the pugnacious qualities of Vorticism as can be seen in some constructivist, mechanistic works such as *Heavy Structures in a Landscape Setting* of 1922 or the 1925 linocut *The engineer, his wife and their family* (reproduced in Normand 2003: 78). In common with other left-wing Scottish artists, writers, and left-wing activists of this era such as Hugh MacDiarmid, McCance's modernism included a political commitment to a progressive, anarchist and international version of Scots nationalism, as promoted in the magazine *The Modern Scot*, the 'Organ of the Scottish Renaissance' (1930-34). In turn, Hugh MacDiarmid, writing as C.M. Grieve, promoted McCance's machine aesthetic as a true reflection of a Scots national character: 'So far there has been too great a cleavage between Engineering and Art. Actually what has taken place in Scotland up to the present is that our best constructive minds have taken up engineering and only sentimentalists have practised art. We are largely (and the world has assessed us rightly) a nation of engineers. Let us realise that a man may still be an engineer and yet concerned with a picture conceived purely as a kind of engine with a different kind of functional power…' ('Contemporary Scottish Studies: William and Agnes McCance' Grieve 1925, cited in Normand 2003).

In tune with these machine dreams, and despite its remoteness, there were some eruptions of technological modernity in Galloway. For example, after the First World War a former wartime aircraft engine production unit at Tongland was refurbished and relaunched as an automobile factory in 1920 with an all-women workforce to produce that daringly liberated vehicle of female mobility, the Galloway 10/20 sports car 'made by ladies for others of their sex' (Worthington-Williams 1995). Several modernising landowners and engineers started to examine Galloway's potential for hydro power in order to develop electricity generation enterprises. Although at first this did not appear to be a commercial proposition in such a sparsely populated region, the passing of the Act to create the Central Electricity Board (CEB) in 1926 created conditions that were favourable to this project. The CEB had

executive powers to construct and operate a national grid and to centralise power generation (Hudson and Hunter 1938: 7; Hannah 1979: 100–104). In this national framework the hydroelectric schemes in South Scotland were seen as an important connecting link in the network between Central Scotland and North West England, while the opportunity of getting subsidies from the Unemployment Grants Committee to support transmission line construction costs provided a further impetus towards realisation. Galloway power could now be exported, via the Central Electricity Board, to industrial and municipal customers in Central Scotland and North-West England. In 1929 the Galloway Water Power Company outlined plans for five power stations, reservoirs and other supporting works with construction work that took place between 1931 and 1936. The appearance of the power stations in this scheme, such as at Tongland, were in accord with avant-garde functional engineered forms of modernism in architecture that were in vogue with Scottish architects of the 1930s (McKean 1987: 6–7). The power station at Tongland was housed in a tall white pillared rectangular structure embellished with simple repeating vertical glazed panels, and surmounted by a looming giant cylindrical form. The calm classical balance of this geometrical simplicity announced a rational control over the unruly forces of nature. The cylindrical structure, for example was a so-called 'surge tower'– designed to damp out and regularise peaks and surges in the mutual flows of water and electricity in this power system (Hawthorne and Williams 1938: 53). Natural flows of living beasts, the mating and migration rushes of salmon, also had to be factored in, with local fishing and sporting concerns and the Inspector of Salmon Fisheries in Scotland represented in the planning and experimental development process of the power stations. Salmon for the Manchester and London markets were a major local product and shipped out by sea direct from Tongland (Donnachie 1971). While the fish ladder at the side of the station as seen in Figure 2 appears as a gentle and unthreatening staircase to the upper reaches of the river, the engineers in charge of the overall power station design tell us a more punishing story about this element of the design. Large fish had to get upstream to spawn, while small immature fish, smolts, had to return again after their first year in fresh water upstream. For smolts passing inadvertently through Tongland power turbines, this meant they would get a 'fair battering' due to rapid pressure changes in the water; first a burst of very high pressure followed by a sudden drop to a 'partial vacuum' at a fraction of atmospheric pressure. The engineers cheerfully reported their investigations and solutions: in the face of the threat of these 'rather unpromising conditions' the fish were experimented on, 'imprisoned in a tank and subjected to the same pressure fluctuations'. As these fish had not apparently taken too much damage from these severe pressure changes, the arrangements for their passage were deemed good to put into operation as it was 'only infrequently that any stunned or injured fish are seen' (Hudson and Hunter 1938: 30–31).

In his book of architectural history, *The Scottish Thirties*, Charles McKean mentions the Glenlee power station at New Galloway briefly as an example of 'workplace architecture' that, he implies, does not deserve longer mention because having been designed by an engineer, Sir Alexander Gibb, it barely rose above the level of a functional shed that foreshadowed 'WW2 military architecture' (McKean 1987: 115). But the modernism of the Galloway hydro scheme was not just to do with the style of individual buildings, nor even about the integrated design processes for managing nature in and around the Dee and Doon river systems. Instead, it was about a willingness to centralise, coordinate and manage whole constellations of physical and organisational infrastructures of financial investment, professional collaboration and government policy. Electrification in the era of the National Grid is an example of a 'system building' approach to the construction of a planned network at regional or national scale (Hughes 1983: 324). This marked a change from the earliest hydro electricity schemes around the turn of the century that had been localised if spectacular capitalist private enterprises, often associated with specific goals of electro-chemical production or mineral extraction. At Loch Ness, for example, the British Aluminium Company began to develop its hydro electrically powered aluminium smelting plant at the Falls of Foyers in 1895 (Payne 1988: 6-11). By contrast, the Galloway scheme was not a profitable single site, but became profitable because of the National Grid. Although smaller in scope, the Galloway scheme was similar in ethos to the Tennessee Valley Authority (TVA), established in the same decade in the US in 1933. This was a celebrated New Deal scheme that was intended, as Julian Huxley described it in 1943, as 'an adventure in planning' encompassing an entire region and a whole gamut of economic infrastructure, that deliberately included hydro electricity, flood control, synthetic fertiliser production, scientific farming, through to the protection and reinstatement of natural woodlands, tourist highways, visitor facilities, and community centres in its scope (Huxley 1943). The TVA's hydro dams provided a central focus for visitors, with

their combination of crafted landscapes of forest and roaring waters with the most austere and geometrical modern architecture and engineering. This sights were extolled as not merely functional, but as part of a new aesthetic order: 'the modern eye can appreciate more easily the beauty in machinery than it can in the fine arts' (Huxley 1943).

But in contrast to the gigantic or sublime scale of the TVA landscape interventions, the Galloway scheme was designed in, and for, a productive, pastoral landscape. Just as the establishment of the Scottish Milk Marketing Board in 1933, another centralised initiative, helped to mitigate the constant instability that had plagued local dairy businesses in this period (Donnachie 1971: 21), so national electrification offered an opportunity for exploiting the energy power of the woods, fields and waters of the region so it could be processed and exported alongside cattle, fish, textiles and other products. The power stations of the Galloway scheme should be viewed not simply as an exercise in architectural Modernism, but instead as an ambitious landscaping scheme to produce an electric pastorale that recalled the engineers' aim, first framed in the late eighteenth century, to work at 'the production and ordering of space in the framework of a rational state' (Picon 1992: 119).

Figure 3: Photograph from *The Galloway Hydro-Electric Development* (1938): Tongland CEB sub-station

Bibliography:

Barrell, John (1980) *The dark side of the landscape: the rural poor in English painting 1730-1840* Cambridge: Cambridge University Press

Donnachie, I. (1971) *The industrial archaeology of Galloway*, The Industrial Archaeology of the British Isles series Newton Abbot: David & Charles

Glendinning, Miles (1997) *Rebuilding Scotland: the postwar vision, 1945-1975* East Linton : Tuckwell

Gold, John R. and Margaret M. Gold (1995) *Imagining Scotland: tradition, representation and promotion of Scottish Tourism since 1750* Aldershot: Scolar Press

Hannah, Leslie (1979) *Electricity before nationalisation: a study of the development of the electricity supply in Britain to 1948* Manchester: Manchester University Press

Harvie, Christopher (1977) *Scotland and nationalism: Scottish society and politics, 1977–1977* London: George Allen & Unwin

Hawthorne, William and Frederick Herbert Williams 'The mechanical and electrical plant' *The Galloway Hydro-Electric Development* Reprint of papers presented to the Institution of Civil Engineers, 22nd February, 1938 London: Institution of Civil Engineers: 45–63

Hudson, William and John Kenneth Hunter 'The constructional works' *The Galloway Hydro-Electric Development* Reprint of papers presented to the Institution of Civil Engineers, 22nd February, 1938 London: Institution of Civil Engineers: 6–42

Hughes, Thomas P. (1983) *Networks of power: electrification in Western society, 1880–1930* Baltimore and London: John Hopkins University Press

Huxley, Julian (1943) *TVA: an adventure in planning* Cheam, Surrey (War Address): The Architectural Press

McKean, Charles (1987) *The Scottish Thirties: an architectural introduction* Edinburgh: Scottish Academic Press

The Modern Scot (J.H. Whyte: Dundee 1930–34)

Nye, David E. (1994) *American technological sublime* Cambridge, Mass.: MIT Press

Normand, Tom (2000) *The modern Scot: Modernism and nationalism in Scottish Art 1928–1955* Aldershot: Ashgate

Payne, Peter L. (1988) *The Hydro: a study of the development of the major hydro-electric schemes undertaken by the North of Scotland Hydro-Electric Board* Aberdeen: Aberdeen University Press

Paxton, R. and Shipway, J. (2007) *Civil engineering heritage: Scotland – Lowlands and Borders*, London: Thomas Telford: 11–14

Penfold, Alastair (1981) *Thomas Telford, 'Colossus of Roads'* Telford: Telford Development Corporation and Ironbridge Gorge Museum Trust

Picon, Antoine (1992) *French architects and engineers in the age of enlightenment* Cambridge: Cambridge University Press

'Tongland Bridge' Canmore online resource of the Royal Commission on the Ancient and Historical Monuments of Scotland (RCAHMS) http://canmore.rcahms.gov.uk/en/site/64106/details/tongland+bridge/&biblio=more accessed 31 October 2013

Ruddock, Ted (2000) 'Telford, Nasmyth and picturesque bridges' in D. Mays, M. Moss and M.K. Oglethorpe, eds *Visions of Scotland's past* East Lothian: Tuckwell Press: 134–144

Telford, Thomas (1838) *Life of Thomas Telford, civil engineer*, edited by John Rickman London: Payne and Foss

Williams, Raymond (1975) *The country and the city* Oxford: Oxford University Press

Worthington-Williams, Michael (1995) 'The Galloway Story' *The Automobile* 13: 70-76

Mitch Miller

THE CLAN MAPS
the CHOSEN FIELD

A journal of a Journal of a Tour of Real Life Scotland

Verb umprin-cipiant through the trancitive spaces! Kilt by Kelt shall kithagain with kinagain. **James Joyce,** *Finnegan's Wake page 306.*

I. Departure

I did not catch *The Real Life Gordons of Huntly,* Ross Sinclair's project at artwork the Deveron Arts Centre in Huntly, which took place over the summer of 2011. Truth be told, I was in that vaguest of excuse-states, 'busy' and did not notice any projects that were not my own. Even had I known, I am not sure I would have taken the road and miles to Huntly. The last time I visited was in 2007, in search of an encampment of Gypsies/Travellers whose young child had been attacked by local men armed with paint-guns. It's fair to say I rather took against the place as a result.

Having read We ♥ Real Life Scotland (the book of the movie, as it were) it is obvious that this (hypothetical) exercise of prejudice on my part would have been entirely my loss. But I would at least be 'on theme'; *The Real Life Gordons* explores the emotional charge tribe and family imbue into settlements, territories and landscapes. The family in question here are the Gordons, powerful notables often in open rebellion to the crown, namesakes of that one dance we all know how to do at a ceilidh, and shorthand for one of more prolific Scottish

regiments. Look for Huntly's location on a clan map and you will find GORDON emblazoned over it. Sinclair (look up a bit on the clan map to see where his lot are…) takes this history as his point of departure, so I will follow suit.

Industrialisation and the pull of the cities have diminished the connections between genealogy and geography into features of graphic design rather than graphic violence. Anne L. Forbes' essay in this volume, hints that if I were a supporter of rival family the Stewarts of Moray, an aversion to Huntly could be well justified. Nowadays, a Stewart need have no fear for himself on *that particular* social basis – but were he to roll into town with trailer in tow, maybe there are still constituencies to avoid. Ultimately there is no such thing as the wrong place, but there is always, potentially, the wrong time.

This negative take is, it should be said, an excrescence entirely of my own making – Sinclair's approach was altogether more inclusive, celebratory and open-minded. *Real Life Scotland* spans over two decades of work. Its 'signature' image is the self-portrait of Sinclair in various situations, 'taps aff' and displaying the 'REAL LIFE' tattoo that stretches between his shoulder blades. Bodily presence is crucial to how he chooses to engage with his subjects and participants, and the lively discussion he initiated over Huntly's clan-map connection to the Gordon name touches upon narratives that run much broader and deeper than any town or city can contain.

Gordons was a happening, a moment where, as his commissioners at Deveron put it, 'the town is the venue'. What Sinclair describes as an 'incidence' means own bodily absence cuts me off from many of its more enriching elements. But Sinclair has provided a book and CD for my benefit. Documenting socially engaged processes loses a lot in translation, but Sinclair has attempted to make this an active 'thing' in its own right. He gives a detailed account of the project, from the first approach by Deveron Arts to take up a theme and see the 'town as the venue' and its people as participants, rather than an audience. To this he has added contributions from these participants, from critics and fellow artists, and even an original essay from the sociologist David McCrone (which alone makes it worth having). This gives the book a sense of its own autonomy and completeness, even if it cannot replicate what it was like to be there. But it also very deliberately makes the reader aware of his or her own position. Either you read this book to remind you of something you were part of, or you weren't there and this book is all you have to go on. If you fall into the second group, then Sinclair has a question for you

Are you the reader, now the audience of this work, a few steps removed – another layer of participants in the process?

It is a very good question that I will attempt to answer – not least because the critical responses Sinclair has already included in his book – from Craig Richardson, Francis McKee and Peter McCaughey – are thorough and astute in teasing out the themes and continuities of Sinclair's 25 years of practice. Driven though it may have been, by *presence*, by *being present* and various performative moments, this is a work of multiple readings (and this, require us to visit at least three different *Real Life* Huntlys). A stack of books greets me on page 4, titles – *Painting the Nation, Landseer, A Life of Walter Scott, Lanark, Burns Collected Poems, The Scottish Song Book – Contralto* and *Kings and Queens of Scotland* are just part of the *Real Life Library of Scotland*. Reading underpinned the project (Sinclair boned up on all 600 years of the Gordon line), and it can bottle the potency of certain moments in time. It can a *la* Walter Scott, alter reality, and even start wars (if you take Mark Twain's word for it).

To reiterate – *I wasn't there* – but with a book and a wealth of experiential ignorance to go on, will forge ahead never the less.

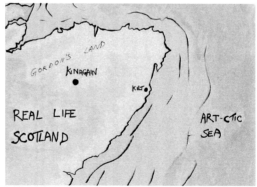

II. Kinagain

People wore their Sunday best,
but it was Saturday.
Ross Sinclair

As I prepare to test my Meta against Sinclair's, it should be noted that my travel guide is a hand-some looking object in it's own right. In Artificial Hells, Claire Bishop grouses over the poor documentation of socially engaged art projects – those who have ploughed though slapdash archiving and fuzzy photographs can sympathise. Not so here. We ♥ Real Life Scotland is full colour, doubles its dust jacket as a poster and is nicely bound and typeset. Given that Sinclair's intention is to dissect, confront and engaged Scotland's relentless creation of images of itself – of fictions that mediate our sense of what has been called (Walter) Scott-Land, giving attention to the book as a form in itself, as a vehicle and tool of deployment, makes perfect sense.

Inside we have a series of essays – or perhaps, more appropriately narratives – representing subjective accounts, local and family histories, satires, reminiscences, sociology and critical accounts. Among them is an American Kim Gordon, head of the US 'clan' whose 'personal view' in notions of blood, belonging and the American hyphenated identity. Anne Forbes' family history of the Gordons is a respectable official history, while the editor of the local paper contributes a couthy, cliché-rich take on Scottishness that perfectly embodies the nature of the Scottish local newspaper. Local historian Patrick Scott provides a solid topographical structure in his 'virtual tour' of Huntly, but it is Darren Sharp's short testimonial that salts the affair with some necessary grit. An ex-serviceman in the Gordons, he is a living example of how long standing and cross-generational allegiance to the Gordon name can be –

> I had served in the 1st Batallion The Gordon Highlanders. My grandfather had also been a Gordon Highlander, and it was this connection that I had grown up with.

'Sharpy' is no *Born on the Fourth of July* conflicted vet and recounts his pride at marching through the streets of his hometown with his regiment, 'bayonets fixed.'

In this 'set list' of essays 'the whole complicated and contradictory paradigm of Scottish history [is] conjured up in glorious microcosm.' The book does much the same for the broader Scottish literary conversation, representing many of the perspectives that have competed, sometimes colluded, to give Scotland its 'given image' of itself. Sinclair's formal choices as author/editor lend weight to Roddy Buchanan's contribution, a thoughtful encomium that makes a…

> call for people to pay closer attention to Ross Sinclair's 'Real Life' projects. It would be a great starting point for any courageous commissioning editor out there. His projects operate on the constructed landscape of the Art World. This is his chosen field. He has picked his way across an art scene that bloomed in Glasgow and grew in the naughties. His work has shown a remarkable continuity and I would argue provides an important case study on how a person's personal

relationship to the political has been valued as a subject for discussion in Scotland and abroad over the last twenty years.

As Buchanan indicates, the Huntly 'incidence' is indeed, just one note in something Sinclair has been playing out over many years, movements and periods. I am not just giving you some flashy prose here; music is both an important constituent activity, and metaphor for Real Life Scotland's interrogation of our myth making impulse. The poster on the dust-jacket is a cheeky 'set list' of the top 20 Scottish Monarchs, rendered in the bold colours and Schipka Pass fonts in his now familiar style. In *Real Life in Auld Reekie* (2013 – which I DID see) the billboards facing the Calton Road back entrance to Edinburgh's Waverley Station were commandeered to parse weighty subjects such as citizenship, drug culture, capitalism, footballers and a certain referendum into handy 10-point lists. These suggested forms for conveying the complex reality of a complex city were repeated in beer mats and postcards spread all over the city. In the Real Life Gordons Sinclair began by researching and producing 'great man' portraits of various Gordon luminaries. These were made into signs and sandwich boards, collated into a carnival-style flashboard display and have a 'Panini' collectible sticker feel that makes them deceptively subversive in form.

Other useful call-backs include the controversial neon signs temporarily installed on Glasgow City Chambers in 2005 (later 'reconstructed' by Peter McCaughey in his Psychic Derives), the dystopian CCA show Real Life Rocky Mountain (1996), and Sinclair vs Landseer (2007). The latter took on the legacy of the Victorian painter whose 1860 work Flood in the Highlands evaded the surfeit of tragedy that created this fictional wilderness in favour of imagined disasters. Craig Richardson is probably on the money in arguing that Sinclair's intervention (a be-neoned, stag-headed Land Rover installed opposite the painting on a slipstream of vinyl) saved the painting from redundancy.

And then those definitive photographs. Each is again, a distinctive note in a single continuity, taking in locations ranging from Orkney to the Glenfiddich Distillery (see The Drouth Issue 37). They stretch back to the germination of Real Life back in 1993 – tableaux of Sinclair's bare back, green and white checked shorts against iconic surroundings. Real Life Gordons generates plenty more, this time as action shots, with Sinclair brandishing one of the portraits he made of notable Gordons as he traverses the town in a sort of faux-protest. Richardson contextualises it as a Rückenfiguren ('Reverse Figure') familiar to anyone who has seen Caspar David Freidrich's Wanderer above the Sea of Fog (1818). Richardson's argument is nuanced and deserves to be followed through blow by blow, but basically, he argues that Sinclair's decision to turn his back to us implicates the viewer after the fact in viewing the scene along with the faceless Sinclair – it stimulates 'our own individual contemplation.'

For Richardson, these artists share more than just a composition. Both ask whether 'we' can we rise above the fog a la the Wanderer, or are condemned to ruminating over mists and fragments? Scottish political commentators tend to see this as the building blocks of the pseudo-country behind Scotland the Brand (as dissected by David McCrone), but what can we say of Real Life, the tattoo?

If the Real Life pose is a Romantic gesture, then it only goes to highlight the tensions that are the stuff of this work – Real Life Scotland may critique Scott and challenge Landseer, but it shares their DNA. And how can you engage your audience to partici-pate when you turn your back to them – tell them to read the legend, not the lived in face of the thing? In The Real Life Gordons Sinclair performed a song (something of a mnemonic of major events in Gordon history – another list, in fact) with his back to the actual real life Gordons he had invited to dine in the grounds of Huntly castle. Richardson may be right to dub this a 'contradictory gesture'

but he also quotes jazz performance traditions whereby the back was turned to the audience so they would concentrate on the notes. In fact, Sinclair himself describes this practice as putting the tattoo 'to the fore'.

And that brings up the issue of, not so much where the bodies are buried, but embodied. Two are implicated here; Sinclair's own, and the body politic into which he places himself. It's another of the transitions, or continuities he threads into his practice, a physical reality, something we can touch, smell, taste and feel (please do ask his permission first) – into something entirely notional, something we can conceive, institute and declare, but never wholly define.

In Real Life Gordons Sinclair constructed a temporary community around the idea of being one of the family. Originally borderers, the Gordons made good in the wars of Independence and were awarded lands in the north. Their fortunes were closely tied to the Stewart dynasty that followed, supporters but ran into trouble when their Catholic beliefs led them into rebellion against James VI. As was typical of aristocratic politics, a last minute switch of sides saved Gordon from the headsman's block and led to promotion as a Marquis. As Gordon's personal narrative peaked and troughed, so Huntly followed suit.

Such was the order of things, and thus, how the history of Huntly has been weighted and crafted for future generations. The question, as David McCrone posits in his essay 'Scotland – the Brand', is what happened when that history inevitably becomes heritage – Heritage, to use the rather feeble English –language equivalent, refers to the panoply of material and symbolic inheritances, designed to meet the needs of the modern age to know 'who we are'.

Heritage is thus, where history collides with social need and in this at least, it parallels art's 'relational aesthetic'. Since Tom Nairn's blistering attack on heritage in The Enchanted Glass the term has been something of a dirty word, especially in the Scottish context. But both McCrone and Sinclair find useful room to manoeuvre within the concept, opportunities to bond that need not be invested in diaspora, or indeed blood.

This makes Sinclair's first intervention, in which he phoned up everyone in Huntly with the Gordon surname to invite them to dinner, particularly interesting.

> We invited them all to come, cajoled and encouraged, asking them to bring mementos and memories of their Gordon heritage/lineage to share and discuss.

In microcosm then, we have a pocket Scotland – an 'imagined community' created out of a proposed shared heritage;

> Through the work one can reflect on questions of identity, what's in a name, what's family, where do we come from and where might we be going? How can we understand and engage with these big issues of identity/geography/history/time/ class/ownership. Maybe in a small way by initiating the dialogue with a kindness.

This dialogue is important and is an important bulwark against the atavism that comes with clan identity. It is Francis McKee who coins the word 'bloodline' which further raises the spectre of the sort of para-paradoelic pattern recognition that keeps conspiracy theorists in such brisk business. What emerges is rather more plural, such as Kim Gordon's focus on ancestry, a world record Scottish country dancing attempt and the unexpected revival of a 'broadside ballad' against the 4th Duke of Gordon's industrial improvements in the early 1800s. Perhaps because it began with a kindness, Sinclair's jerry-built clan is surprisingly dissonant and inclusive. Rather than blood and belonging, the project created a shared 'poetic image' of the 'Gordons'. Like the phenomenon described by

the philosopher Bachelard, these images are 'reverberates' through old archetypes by artists to re-describe our present. It seems a serviceable description of what happened at Huntly.

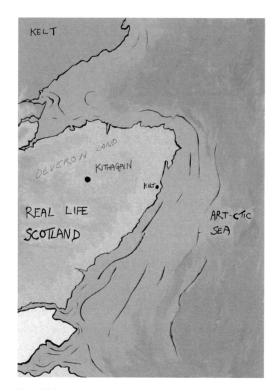

III. Kithagain

Darren Sharp's testimony is particularly important to understanding The Real Life Gordons, not for its ecumenical qualities (which were many) but the project's willingness to rile up and disrupt. Sharpy's personal heritage raises the spectre of those Kelts that Kilt for the empire, an uncomfortable fit with the left-liberal tendencies of the Art World. Turnabout being fair play, Sinclair places his portrait of enlisted-man 'Sharpy' in the same style and sequence as Robert the Bruce and various Lords and Marquises, and a deliberate contrast with the many portraits of the Gordon Highlander's officer class.

And so, quietly, almost nonchalantly, Sinclair 'does a Benjamin' and calls the past forth into the present, not so much as heritage, but as the dialectical image of Sharpy, replete with problems, contradictions and conversations that threaten to grow increasingly polite. That they do not seem to have done so in Huntly may owe a lot to the same impulse that is doubtless, prompting many families to avoid discussing a certain referendum at the dinner table.

One of the wonderful – and weird – things about the space socially engaged projects open up is exactly this sort of strange-bedfellow diversity, threatened, yet possibly sustained by its internal tensions.

The three examples Sinclair gives in his account – the Gordon's get together at Huntly, Real Life's attendance of the agricultural fair and the mobile museum – show different ways of taking on the question of what a 'we' might be, and how inculcating a sense of shared heritage works to make that function (especially when the sense of family is – that word again – largely notional).

The second example, Real Life Artist in Residence took place at the Huntly Hairst agricultural fair.

I sat there all day painting away (with the help of Ross H. Frew) and making music with my back to the audience as usual, Real Life Tattoo to the fore.

With artist Gayle Meikle explaining the project at the front, Sinclair felt 'like one of the exotic rare breed animals in the show'. Recalling his earlier show – , Sinclair puts himself in a marketplace in a position that aims be both absurd, and challenging, shifting the theme from medieval notions of blood and belonging to a far more modern emphasis on trade, commerce and marketable skills – Can culture and art be just another aspect of what goes on in this town, within this community?

The third example was again, a seemingly tongue in cheek exercise but surreptitiously, rather serious. The project inverted the museum tour – it gathered a group of them as was willing (40 in all, apparently from all walks of life – pun intended), distributed artefacts and expositional objects and led this group of locals, visitors, tourists and arty types in beating the bounds over the course of a summer's evening.

It was at this event that Sharpy was presented with his portrait, Anne Forbes stood at the front of Huntly castle and delivered the official history of the Gordons, local archaeologist Colin Shepherd made an unadvertised interception armed with seditious ballad and Patrick Scott delivered a potted history of his town (and his subject) from atop a park bench.

> Perhaps we could bask together in the warm g low of an ambiguous grasp on a factual history of the Gordons in Huntly, in Scotland, in Europe etc, and begin to reconstruct it in a more common, enquiring manner.

Just and fine sentiments, but one wonders if indeed, this project has created something of a 'commons' through which this history – and perhaps, this heritage – can be appraised. Or did it have its commons on that summer's night in Huntly?

An essay I have yet to mention has potentially, a great deal to say on all the themes and subjects raised by what Sinclair does, has done, and has here written. Lane Relyea of Chicago Northwestern University describes Sinclair's own (apparent) group allegiance to perceived 'generation' of Glasgow School of Art graduates (mostly from the Environmental Art Course) who studied, collaborated and conversed with each other over the late eighties and nineties. Ever the student of group formation, Sinclair staged a portrait of himself and his contemporaries after the Life magazine photograph of New York School artists protesting neglect of their work. Surrounded by a gilt frame, Relyea describes Irascibles as self-critique that was nevertheless, short of being a complete self-parody, replete with enough assertiveness and swagger to create an enduring narrative.

Sinclair stands alongside Karen Vaughan, Douglas Gordon, Christine Borland, Jackie Donachie, Malcolm dicksaon Nathan Coley, Helen Nugent and contributors Roddy Buchanan and Richardson, a decent percentage of today's Scottish art world, names that have done a great deal to shape it. Their reputation is founded on art made through conversation, mutual help and dialogue. As Buchanan remembers, the group lived in each other's pockets and on each others couches, helping paint a mural here, knocking a nail or two in there. So close were many of these relationships that the time honoured phrase 'reader – she married him/her' is the only thing that really covers it.

Why does Sinclair include this seeming diversion ? It is admittedly, useful background, telling the reader where Sinclair is from, what he's up to. But it is hard not to conclude that there is also self-analysis here. This is, we are told, a generation –and as any Bible reader will tell you, a generation is also a clan.

So the Irascibles are themselves a cluster of notional Gordons (up to and including Douglas Gordon, who is also of course, actually, a Gordon). I do not mean to cast aspersions, or diminish the individual agency or autonomy of these artists – far from it. Their teacher David Harding has spoken of the family feeling that bound the group together and gave them drive and purpose.

Perhaps it is time we rehabilitated clannishness, and acknowledge that there are multiple identities nestled within our own. I may name-check Sinclair as a catch all for a many-handed project up at Deveron, but were I to say that there are elements of Buchanan, Borland, and Gordon mixed up in his own chemistry, I'm not sure he'd object. I rather think he pointed it out in the first place.

As an idea of who we are and how we operate, clannishness and its solidarities has its dangers, but compares favourably to the bourgeois myth of the solitary artist-hero, powering himself above the masses on bootstrap self-sufficiency. Bolstered by capital and the art market, this particular 'given image' makes the social dimension clandestine and unsurprisingly, curdles into actual nepotism. It is in no way, Real Life.

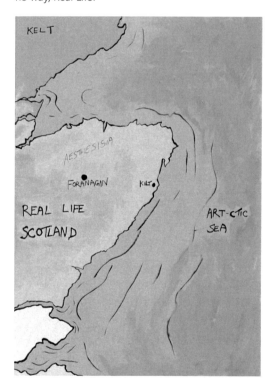

IV. Foranagin (Terminus)

Where's the gap that exists in the market of our imaginations that necessitates something called art to fill it?
Ross Sinclair

It is likely that We ♥ Real Life Scotland will be read not just as a piece of art documentation, but as an important contribution to the debate on the nature of socially engaged art. Most contemporary artists integrate self reflection into their work, it comes with the proverbial territory (more accurately, it IS a proverbial territory) but Sinclair, perhaps prompted by the gentle obstructions and provocations laid in his path by Deveron, gives it particular attention here. Interspersed in his personal account, and implied in many of the others, are observations, tentative conclusions and, probably most germane of all, further questions.

His timing is apt. Historians of Socially Engaged Art such as Nato Thompson trace its origins to the early nineties, just as Sinclair and his contemporaries were starting their professional careers. Glasgow's DIY art scene, the close social ties between its artists and the broader situation of the city, made it a natural breeding ground for socially engaged work. New social movements such as the Free University Network and to a much lesser extent, Workers City, brought artists (most of the Irascibles, and from the older generation the likes of Alasdair Gray and James Kelman) together with activists to organise conferences and mount campaigns. Glasgow was not unique in this – there were many parallels in Europe and the Americas – but it seems a natural, unforced outgrowth of existing traditions.

When Sarah Lowndes titled her history of the Glasgow Art Scene Social Sculpture, it touches upon the move in art practice away from shaping materials extracted from the world into products and productions, towards an interest in the processes surrounding those productions. The structures, institutions and social fabric that surround such processes become in itself, plastic elements to be shaped and remodelled.

This places the artist in a powerful position, as enabler and instigator, whose presence is arguably, what allows these processes to be art. There are many resulting ironies. The socially engaged artist wants to work collectively, yet the position they occupy potentially bolsters their mystique and power – not least because they often retain the best, and clearest sense of how everything fits together. At Huntly Hairst point Sinclair kept collaborator Gayle Meikle to frame the project for passers by – at least in terms of what they thought the project was. This open-endedness opens up considerable potential, but can leave the field open to power plays and sloppy practice.

And then there is the paradox implied by Boris Groys's essay, The Loneliness of the Project, which declares in its opening salvo that 'The formulation of diverse projects has now become the major preoccupation of contemporary man'. Its dark side is a form of contemporary, sanctioned hermitage;

> It is commonly accepted that writing a book, preparing an exhibition or striving to make a scientific discovery are pastimes that permit the individual to avoid social contact, to discommunicate, if not to excommunicate himself – yet without automatically being judged to be a bad person.

So is a socially engaged project, premised on conversation, involvement and dialogue, actually an excuse for Ross Sinclair to isolate himself in 'desirable and socially legitimate loneliness'? Is it about licence to live 'life in the project', with no product in mind, and aims so vague even the process of documenting what you are doing is pointless – and to be avoided?

The anxieties Groys identifies are taken up in the growing critical literature on social engagement. Nato Thompson released a compendium-cum-history at about the same time as We ♥ Real Life Scotland and Bourriaud, who defined the relational aesthetic to which socially engaged art is indebted, got in early with Postproduction (2001). But the most influential is Claire Bishop's Artificial Hells (2010) a rigorous – at times rather harsh, history of 'the social turn' intended as a corrective as perceived drift into on the one hand, toothlessness, and on the other, becoming sociology or social work by default.

Admittedly, there are a number of socially engaged art projects that are mostly feel-good measures to increase gallery numbers and fulfil those wonderfully Blairite fudges 'impact' and 'participation'. Sinclair himself notes that

> I think of course, the responsibility of the artist in this context is to make sure the projects they develop are on balance, first and foremost art-works that mixed audiences/participants rather than simply entertainment or diversion, especially in the often robust shadow of funding imperatives and a bums on seats demand/mentality of post project reports and review.

As a hybrid form that naturally draws upon ethnography, anthropology, education and even social work in its operations, the possibilities of drift towards becoming an actual social programme, losing all sense of the aesthetic form of the piece and closing down the very openness and possibility that makes social practice so attractive, is equally real.

> In insisting upon consensual dialogue, sensitiv-ity to difference, it risks becoming a new kind of repressive norm – one in which artistic strategies of disruption, intervention or over-identification are immediately ruled out as 'unethical' because all forms of authorship are equated with authority and indicted as totalising.

Bishop argues that she is not here to castigate but re-calibrate, from the dominance of ethical concerns back towards the aesthetic. The aesthetic needs to have its day right enough, but Bishop's intended pole shift is not without its own problems.

For one, her notion of ethics is rather fixed, and lags behind some of the latest pertinent developments in this field. At times, her account threatens to diminish the continuing relevance of ethical problems in this field. What for example, is the authority of the artist to disrupt a community – especially if they will not necessarily face the consequences of this disruption alongside that community, having since departed?

Ethics needs to keep pace with the new aesthetics being created by projects such as Real Life Gordons. I have just finished a project which brought together a major museum with a marginalised community in which the effects of artistic intervention were so obvious. Our concern had been to minimise the extent to which our project reproduced the complex internal politics of the community. What we did not realise was that our art project was in itself a Maguffin, around which the politics of that community were re-oriented and, you could argue, somewhat distorted. Luckily, we noticed, and measures were taken. If we had not. done so, then our creative disruptions could have become poisonous

I raise this not to wag the finger but to underline just how many questions this sort of work creates – and their wide ranging, transitive importance. As a Real Time account of how a knowledgeable and perceptive practitioner faces down these questions, *We ♥ Real Life Scotland* is a valuable source text not of answers, but of questions we can collectively explore in the territory between here, there and Real Life.

Ross Sinclair and Others, (2012) *We ♥ Real Life Scotland*, Deveron Arts, Huntly

Raymond Burke

CLOSE

Flat 32

I don't know why I decided to look out of the window.

Daytime telly was numbing me. Even though I had come to loathe the extravagant dullness of quiz and chat within the first couple of weeks, I still caught myself glaring into the void. Every day. It didn't get any better. Going online was the same. Don't know what I'm searching for and end up on facebook with nothing to say. Looking at the blank box and praying for inspiration whilst being bombarded by be-nice-to-puppies chain posts or distant temporally tenuous friends showing off how much they cared about everything from autism to endangered armadillos. How come nobody gives a fuck about scrapheap man? So it was either daytime telly or the window. No competition. Two floors up and a cloudy summer's day meant that that the window was always much more interesting. However, I had decided to ration myself to one scan every hour at the most. Just in case the neighbours thought I was a bit mental.

I stood up and shuffled over for a quick scan with hunched shoulders and my hands tucked comfortably into my pockets. There was a row of four shops facing the flat. Apparently, when first built, there had been a grocer, a butcher, a fruit shop and a Post Office. How could the town planners have got it so wrong? Now we had a Chinese take away, a hairdresser's, a bookies and a licensed newsagent. That's what the people wanted. Within a generation we had caught up with every other scheme in the West of Scotland. Our local shops were now the throbbing heart of a community of fat, drunk gamblers with nice hair.

I hadn't looked out since the half-nine dug: our street's version of the one o'clock gun. I never realised that the half-nine dug even existed until recently; I would usually have been at work by that time. But now, half nine on the dot every day and the yelping would start for about five minutes until the owner came back out of the newsagent. I took the opportunity of being in the newsagent one day at the correct time and hinted to the owner that his dog was a bit annoying for people in the flats. He hinted that I should fuckin' flit.

There wasn't much happening in the street below. The furniture from one of the sub-lets in the next block was being bundled up on the front lawn. The bloke who runs the cargo shop now owns half the flats in the street. Always someone moonlighting. Always a bundle of cheap crap waiting to be picked up. Always a fuckin' mess.

In front of the newsagent sat a large flower planter overflowing with litter, next to a council litter-bin with a very small tree growing through a crack in the tarmac underneath. Very few people about. One old lady standing outside the hairdresser with lumps of silver paper all over her head and a towel round her neck was having a fag opportunity whilst whatever they have done to her hair took effect. An old geezer was waving a couple of young lads away. Probably asking him to jump in. Quite right, mate.

Don't look as if you've got many jumps left. Bit early for a bevvy anyway, lads.

Then I noticed someone standing in the doorway of the Chinese.

He was wearing the kind of clobber I found disgusting. Why did people dress like that? Perhaps they thought it looked smart. Perhaps they imagined it gave them a degree of individuality. But to me it just made them disappear into the ever-increasing crowd of vacuous nobodies. Probably referred to himself as a dude.

Arsehole.

Why is he hanging around there? The Chinese doesn't even open for at least another four hours. Maybe he was an unemployed bouncer; just trying to keep his hand in. Had he nothing better to do? How long had he been there? He pulled out his mobile and started to talk, walking a few paces forward and sitting against the bin. He lifted his head as a deep tinkling tune started at the end of the street and an ice cream van appeared. The van pulled up directly in front of where he was standing; obscuring him with a badly painted Scooby Doo.

Why the fuck do we need an ice cream van if we've got a shop?

I continued grimacing at the back of the van for a few minutes wondering who painted it and hoped the person in charge of drawing wasn't in charge of making the ice cream. Maybe that's what he had been up to – waiting on the van. He looked like the van type. Some people don't use ice cream vans: see them as infantile. I waited for him to appear at either side but he remained out of sight. A few of kids came and went and one woman who obviously needed sixty fags and a bottle of Irn Bru.

Then, when the van finally pulled away, the dude was standing in the same position but staring directly at my window. Why? Why was he looking in this direction? He kept staring. He obviously saw me but I didn't want to acknowledge I was looking back at him. I don't know why not. It was my window. I've got more right to look out that he has to look

in. But he remained frozen: staring straight at me. I took my right hand out of my pocket and pretended to scratch at an imaginary mark on the glass whilst keeping my eyes on him. No difference. I kept scratching away at nothing for a few seconds but knew I couldn't keep it up for much longer. I made a big show of looking along the street for a few seconds as if something had caught my attention. But when I turned my eyes back towards him, he was in exactly the same position.

I stepped backwards out of sight.

What did I do that for? I've given up possession of my own window. But I can't go back now. Not for a couple of minutes. I wanted to sit down but I stayed glued to the spot. Somebody on the telly was trying to sell me funeral insurance. I thought about closing the blinds. But that would make me look a bit para. I would just wait.

After a few seconds, I gave up and gradually leaned forward looking over the edge of the frame. I took a small step. Then another. The roof of the shops appeared and the street slowly started to fill the window again. The brightly coloured shop signs and windows came into view and finally – the bin he had been standing next to.

Gone.

I moved a little more quickly now, taking care to check the trees and bushes and parked cars and discarded furniture in case he was trying to hide. Nothing. I moved right up to the window to check the garden underneath. All clear. I closed my eyes, took a deep breath and exhaled all the tension from my lungs before stepping back into the room towards the door. That was close. I leaned my back against the living room wall and stared at the ceiling.

Brrzzd.

The intercom rattled in the hall behind me. I grabbed my remote control and muted the telly before resuming my position, back to the wall. The intercom stopped and after a second another started buzzing somewhere else in the building. Maybe someone had pressed mine by mistake. The buzz stopped quickly and after a few seconds another. No reply. Must have been number twenty eight or new people at thirty. They'll be at work. Then yet another buzz. Then nothing. Whoever it was had given up or had been let in. I was tempted to go and look through the spyhole in the front door but people can tell if you are there. I remained still and listened. The doorbell rang. Twice. I stayed still.

After a few seconds, I heard the letterbox opening and could feel someone staring through.

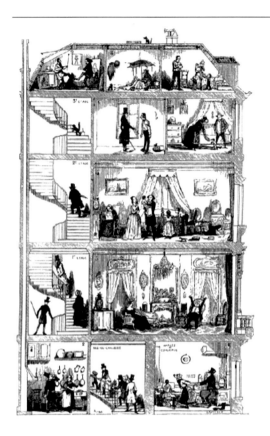

I was well out of sight and tried unsuccessfully to breathe more slowly. Not a sound came from the hall. The letterbox was still open. I could hear him listening. What if I need to go to the loo? I'd have to cross the hall. How could I get into the kitchen? I can't just stay in this room forever. Silence. An old film was starting. Lots of backstory rolling upwards in black and white. I hated that. Couldn't make out the words anyway. I turned my gaze back to the ceiling and waited.

Silence.

I counted at least two minutes but lost my place.

Someone breathing.

'Are you gauny answer this fuckin' door or whit?'

On Listening...

Stephen Davismoon

Music's evocation of place, identity and memory – an artist's perspective

I wish to offer you – as **my Listener** (that critical but all too often overlooked role – after all where would any of us be without those special folk that put aside time to listen, truly listen to us (how was it that Luigi Nono put it?… *'It is very difficult to listen to others in silence. When one listens, one often attempts to find ourselves in others… instead of hearing others, often one hopes to hear oneself ')*)…
I digress; again, I would like to extend to you – **my dear auditor** – an invitation: let us attempt to excavate beyond the mannered, in order that we might encounter ideas of authenticity in creative communication through music.

Such investigations and reflections are important for me to conduct from time to time because I feel that if authenticity is absent from a piece of music, it will always struggle to function as a work of art, since it will – for all intents and purposes – be completely lacking that that Walter Benjamin so famously described as 'aura.'

It is my hope that you will find at least some of what I have to say in the lines that follow to be of some interest, even if just for you to celebrate a little, our ability for focused and informed audition. An act which profoundly expands our understanding of the world around us – its depths, distances, directions, weather, terrain as well as the accents, customs and histories of all its peoples.

In some senses what I have to say to you during our quest, is a little serious in nature, and I feel that I should perhaps apologise a little to you for this, before we embark. Why the apology? Well, perhaps I am being unjustly presumptuous here but it seems evident that the vast majority of one's interface with music or sound art is generally for the purpose of entertainment and enthrallment. This is not to say that I do not find music to be entertaining; of course I do, nor do I here wish to deny its mysterious power to captivate; it holds me under its spell regularly, every day of my life.

What I would like to bring into our midst as we journey, is the idea of music as a form of knowledge. This notion is of course nothing new, it goes back at least to the time of Pythagoras, was championed by early astronomers via the ideas of *Musica Universalis* or the music of the spheres; and theologians (the ideas of St. Gregory led to the development and standardization of a chant form that remains vital more than 14 centuries after his death) – it continued to occupy a vitally important throughout the history of western philosophy up until the late 19th-century (perhaps reaching a 'zenith' in the 'Will' of Schopenhauer) and has maintained critical currency through the many guises of Poststructuralism (Umberto Eco, Claude Levis-Strauss and Gilles Deleuze). More latterly, through an ever-growing body of fascinating work across the fields of psychology (John Sloboda), cognitive science (Stephen McAdams and Albert Bregman) and Artificial Intelligence (Eduardo Reck Miranda) we are beginning to re-capture the objective that music tells us something deeply insightful about what it means to be human.

So, as a reminder, as we now take our first steps, what I would like for us to focus upon during our journey's various stages is the presence and integral

importance of 'authenticity' or 'aura' in music. I'll be talking to you from the perspective of a composer whose primary aims are to create music for performers to engage with and for listeners to become immersed by, hopefully without any sense of mannered falsity. With this in mind I will highlight aesthetic considerations over the technical; as an artist rather than as a musicologist or theorist – although there will be many perspectives alluded to from that other land to aid our vantage points as we go.

Authenticity for me, in the music that I compose, is reflected by a direct connectivity to and expression of the 'realness' of existence – sensually and intellectually – contemplative of life's unfolding, here and now. By recognising the profound importance of the location and identity of a work and mindful as to how it might interface with my memory and that of the musicians and listeners it may engage, it is hoped that I can rather more aptly guard myself from emitting creative lies to my fellow life passengers.

I might point out that our discussions have for me, a practical and somewhat selfish end for the fluency of my own work. Let me explain a little. Often, when I encounter a situation of creative impasse, stalemate or dead-end, after some reflection it often dawns upon me that I have come to occupy such a frustrating, inexpressive corner, because my focus on matters of authenticity and aura have been out of balance somehow. In other words I have not really been thinking about the place that the composition inhabits, the identity that it is expressive of nor the memories that it will intersect with. So I value this opportunity to remind myself of these important issues very much and I thank you in advance for your patience as you listen. As an aside, in my many years of teaching composition, I have been confronted along the way with many students saying things like "I don't know where to go next" or "I don't know where this piece is going to" – again often with a little attention to the work's authenticity and aura many problems seem to be readily solvable. It is as if, once the piece becomes properly located; once its identity and that of the composer becomes more focused and how the work in question will network with the memories of its listeners its poetic purpose finds new and more defined *telos*.

You are right we have been walking a little while now and have not really been taking in the sights. Fair enough let us pause here for a moment and take in the air – listening to the sound of our in – and exhalations. While we pause I'd like to briefly suggest how a work of music lacking authenticity or aura might appear to us – otherwise you could very well ask what is the point of any further effort in our excursion. Well, let us consider a work that is high in derivation so much so that it lacks any sense of location or expressive identity with the author, this could be regarded as such an instance. Where the practitioner through whatever external force can be thought of as a purveyor of a reductive or 'received' expressive palette, which can appear somehow dislocated or inauthentic in relation to the author. Now, I need to be clear here, I am not criticising the wish for anyone to imitate anybody else at all, this can be fun and enjoyable, however I do believe that creative, expressive and thereby cultural problems might arise if this becomes the **only acceptable format or model** for music expression, since it cannot allow the artist in question to meaningfully engage with his or her immediate location, identity and time of living, on their own terms.

Alternatively, and in many senses at the other extreme of this example, a musical work that lacks authenticity or aura could also be one that makes no attempt whatsoever to engage with any previous musical modes of expression (i.e. a 'year zero hypothesis'). As keen as I am on some of the most experimental of computer musics, I can't help but feel that the plethora of ideas for musical formal structuring demonstrated at recent computer music conferences will never, I believe, travel beyond their own culturally limited *cul de sac*. I think that this will prove to be the case in the main because they have chosen – often willfully – not to engage with music's rich and diverse communicative histories. I hope that you will understand then that I am neither proposing musical conservatism nor a year zero cultural hypothesis, but simply to be mindful of music's evocative and communicative potentialities, and their importance in the creation of an authentic musical work.

I think of the aura or authenticity in my creative practice as having at least three – in many senses – overlapping stages or facets which are in a state of constant flux and renewal:

place or location (this can be 'real/concrete' or one that is alluded to);

identity (individual or collective) and *memory* (calling upon networks from the near instantaneous to the atavistic).

I agree let's move on and let's see where the next turn in our path takes us. The presence of these aspects is, in my opinion, keenly felt in the musical works of many musicians from the past and of the present. From Bach to Bob Marley; from John Coltrane to Luigi Nono; from John Cage, to Hank Williams or Iannis Xenakis to Radiohead. When these planes of authenticity are lacking in the

music that I find myself listening to, I begin to sense a coarseness or triteness arise, along with an expressive dishonesty or superficiality in what I am hearing.

I would like now, if you'll allow, to begin the unfurling of each of these 3 layers, suggesting musical models and philosophical perceptions for our illustration along the way. Despite their complex interrelationships (which can give rise to interesting creative nuance) I find it useful – instructional even – to think of them as having a near-linear relationship. For example, if I am having problems with the 'identity' of the piece that I am composing perhaps it is because its 'location' needs to be more focused; after all is it even possible to express or perceive an identity without first sensing or cognising an appropriate expression of place, whether real or imagined? Furthermore, without a sense of place or identity what, if any, memory or memories (singular or networked) can be truly evoked for the listener? This trinity of considerations forms the fundamental aesthetic set that underlies and underpins all of the poietic levels of my creative work – irrespective of the medium that I am working with or what technical preoccupations the work poses.

May we pause for a moment against this wall upon which I often enjoy to rest my arms, in summer time I enjoy to feel the warmth of its bricks. While we take some respite I'd like to invite you to ponder the first of these levels: What **place** or places can be evoked by music?

Let us be sure from the outset if a piece of music evokes a specific place for you today it will never evoke EXACTLY the same place again, ever; a similar place yes perhaps, but because its initial audition will immediately enter into your network of other musically evoked or experienced places, it will instantly become transformed and 'known' within the inner landscape of your imaginings. On hearing the same musical evocation a 2nd, 3rd or nth time will continuously cause it's aura to shift and transform as it interconnects with your other remembered places.

Let's take Richard Strauss' *Alpine Symphony* for a moment, the physical geographic location evoked in this piece is very much extant, however the work's complexities and richness allow for a mobility of listening almost immediately. This mobility of listening becomes further augmented once you have listened to other works inspired by similar locations, (i.e. perhaps Mahler or early Webern) and/ or once you have physically experienced the musical vernacular of the region at first hand. Returning to the same Strauss work for subsequent auditions after such other experiences, you will sense that the locative images that the piece conjured up with its first listen will seem to have transformed and shifted somehow; gained a deeper context or perspective.

Alternatively we could draw similar conclusions from Edgar Varese's early musical representation of an urban/metropolitan environment at the dawn of the 20th Century in his *Ameriques*. Certainly its textural simultaneity allows repeated listenings to remain as vibrant. Our understanding of its location becomes of course further informed when we are able to compare it with other hymns to early urbanity: those by Georges Antheil; Erik Satie; Charles Ives etc. The work's sense of place transforms once again, before our ears so to speak, once we are able to compare it to the soundscapes of the urban metropolitan centres of the 21st century that we experience everyday. The location of Varese and our own is informed by each other, locked in a beautiful chain of feedback.

Let us reflect for a moment as to where we all live, not just you and I and our families, but all of the persons that we have ever come to know and all of their friends and families. Fundamentally, we all live on a clump of land somewhere either close to or surrounded by the delicious flow of water.

If we tilt the perspective of our view of where we all live, to see the broader picture if you will – we of course reside on one huge (mostly blue) globe floating through (eternally dark) space. In the early part of our conversation today you may recall my mentioning to you about *The Music of the Spheres*. Is this perhaps the ultimate locative expression through music?

When one considers that the overriding driver in the development of polyphony in music was to develop a metaphor (or in some cases an attempt to replicate) the movement of the heavenly bodies and the deistic ordering of the cosmos – can one imagine a more fundamental place to be evoked by music; other than the universe within which we all live – listening to a Medieval or Renaissance motet once consciously mindful of this poetic and poietic ambition will never allow me to experience the same listening place ever again; it is at once and forever changed. Have you had the opportunity to listen to the *hope* expressed through the extraordinarily complex heavenly metaphor of Thomas Tallis' in his *spem in alium*? – surely one of the most radical of musics ever to emanate from the broad flatlands in the East of England.

Since ancient times (at least since the times of Pythagoras) musical meditations inspired by the ever-changing heavens have continued to engage the expressive imagination of composers to the present day: through Gustav Holst and Iannis Xenakis, whose *Pleiades* brings a different perspective to the location of the seven sisters.

Let's now pass from this place and move on, while we do so I'd like to ask you to think about what was the first sound that we all heard in our first place?

It would seem more than plausible that, as R. Murray Schafer reminds us ... *it was the caress of the waters [..] in the watery womb of our mother [...] As the ear of the fetus [...] is tuned to the lap and gurgle of water*. The musical evocations of watery places throughout the ages have been numerous: from Monteverdi (to accompany Orpheus as he traverses the lonely waters in search of his beloved Euridice), through to Handel's music commissioned for the 18th century Royal pageant along the Thames through to the pastorale evocations of Beethoven or the Symbolic and Dreamlike melismatic incantations of Debussy and Takemitsu respectively.

All of this talk of water is making me thirsty, perhaps we could stop off somewhere for some sustenance from our excursion? From this early fetul experience onward, it would seem that we continuously use our ears and analytical listening abilities to assist us in the cognition and recognition of our environment during our every waking instant. As so tellingly discussed by Albert Bregman. Within the pages of his *Auditory Scene Analysis*, he also illustrates how our innate complex listening ability allows us to stream sonic information and choose between what is important to us and what is 'noise' or interference; to quite astonishing levels of delicacy.

This looks like a fine place to stop for a beverage what would you like? As I leave you for a moment I'd like to just like to posit a thought with you, so wonderfully expressed by our friend R. Murray Schafer: *no 2 raindrops sound alike*.

Please, here's your water, what a beautiful sound it made as it was being poured from the tap. Now where was I, ah yes musical evocations of climate ... yes well while I am at it there are the musical evocations of snowy, windy and thunderous locations by Jean Sibelius (whose 6th Symphony apparently was like the scent of the first snow), Benjamin Britten (*Peter Grimes*) and Luc Ferarri [*Presque Rien*] – I just say all of this so that we remain mindful of the fact that the weather changes how we hear our environment, quite literally it changes its tuning and alters how it sounds and resonates – think about it for a moment.

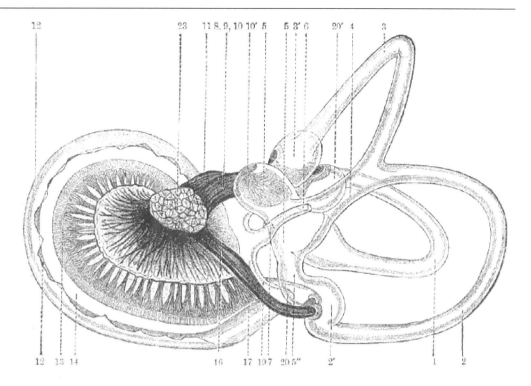

Now, we touched upon music from mountainous regions earlier in our discussions, but how about the musical evocations of Deserts (Steve Reich) wetlands (Vaughan Williams' Norfolk Broads) or the seemingly endless stretches of the Russian Steppes as expressed by Dimitri Shostakovich. Again let's remind ourselves that the topography of our surroundings alters how and what we hear. Even the atavistic evocations expressed in Stravinsky's 'le sacre du printemps' were deeply affected by the surrounding natural landscape of the place and (rather more tellingly perhaps) the rhythms of the birdsong of the region of its composition (as discussed by Francois-Bernard Mache).

The liquid is cool and fresh isn't it, ah the sound of drinking.

Let's now consider some of the other places that are central to our lives/cultures in one sense or another that have regularly found musical expression throughout history. How about musical evocations of places at specific times of day or seasons of the year – whether through the conjuring of naturalistic or manmade 'soundmarks' – the instances are manifold: Vivaldi's *4 Seasons*; John Cage's *The Seasons*; Wagner's *Dawn* in *Gotterdamurung*; Debussy's *Prelude a l'apres d'un faune*; Schoenberg's *Verklarte Nacht*.

Let's remember that our environment sounds or is tuned differently also depending upon the season or time of day for a whole host of reasons.

How about places of worship, work, play and travel each of these locations have all given musical topic to countless musical works including, Messiaen's *Vingt Regards sur l'Enfant Jesus*, Luigi Nono's *La Fabricca Illuminata*, Stravinsky *Petrushka* and Steve Reich's chilling *Different Trains*.

Jean-Jacques Nattiez, Kofi Agawu, Raymond Monelle and many others have of course offered us much about the musical representation and topic presentation of such soundmarks, as well as to how musical evocations of place can culminate to aid the development of our sense of identity. It would seem reasonable to argue that without the evocation of a place the journey towards the creation of a **musical identity** – which is what I would like to move on to next – would lack foundation somehow.

Simon Frith has said of **identity**: *…identity is mobile, a process not a thing, a becoming not a being; …that our experience of music – of music making and music listening – is best understood as an experience of this self-in-process. Music, like identity, is both performance and story, describes the social in the individual and the individual in the social, the mind in the body and the body in the* *mind; identity, like music, is a matter of both ethics and aesthetics.*

So in short musical identity should be seen as a process that grows with us. It should never be seen as static nor reducible but always dynamic. A musical identity is always in flux, as is the case of course with every other sense of identity and as are our ideas of place for that matter.

How is it though that music can work towards the formation of an identity? As Simon Frith has pointed out, the correlations between musical expression and the cultures and sub-cultures that they represent are never straightforward. Probably one of the most fundamental providers of musical identity is through the act and practice of chant. The performance of chant is certainly found the world-over; existing in many cultures as a fundamental binding musical structure.

In many cases chant accompanies sacred ritual. The differing rhythmic inflections, intonations and modes often add further depth and context to continental, national or regional identities. Of course chants aren't always for the fulfillment of sacred ritual, they can accompany many other civic functions: political, work, national, sporting, eating and drinking chants exist across all borders. The bonding power and communal benefits of chanting together in unison with your fellow citizens has been commented upon extensively for centuries if not millennia. Their particular accents, rhythmic nature and intonation give further context to the identity of the chanters – expressive of their place and drawing upon their collective memories and histories.

Shall we move on from this place of refreshment now? If we pass down towards that bridge beside the desolate warehouse our journey will be spent for today. I wonder, can music be expressive of human character ideals/identity values? Or passions (certainly Jean-Jacques Rousseau thought so). How about musical expression of Courage? Justice? Compassion? Certainly composers as diverse as Byrd, Dallapiccola and Nigel Osborne seem to have thought/think so (amongst many others).

The process of the development and 'becoming' of our identity has, with the emergence of the Postmodern condition taken on a whole new sense of acceleration, diffuseness and complexity. Let's think for a moment about what diverse musical lands and times we can now be exposed to during the living of a single day through the hyper-availability of seemingly endless musical search spaces. Just contemplate now the many 'other' collective identities/memories/histories from the world's different regions, nations, continents of our world that we can access at almost any given instant. Such identity diffuseness can be found in Stockhausen's *Telemusik* – an attempt to place the whole of the world's musical practice into a single work!!

The ways in which this hyper-reality is affecting our identity and in turn our memory are of course still being played out.

Just pass down this path towards our left now if you don't mind … yep that's right – so many evenings I spent over there in that enclosure rehearsing my cup final goals – the sound of the ball bouncing on the tarmac, being kicked hard against that metal fence, accompanied by running feet chasing me.

During the closing straight of our walk together, which I have enjoyed tremendously by the way I would like to explore the third layer of my idea of creative authenticity – that of **memory**.

As intimated previously, the development of our identities – musical and otherwise – takes time. Their growth is affected and informed by each new experience. Each new musical experience has a transformative power on those previously received. And on the process goes, it would seem *ad infinitum*.

For musical identities to transform through the channels of our memory we need musical figures or ciphers to be placed upon and within a dynamically networked canvas of time. At this juncture it would seem reasonable to remind ourselves that without a sense of place, a convincing sense of identity or identities is difficult to imagine; and in turn a dynamic sense of identity – one that develops and grows over time – is impossible to conceive without a dynamic network of memories that interconnect and alter over time.

Much has been written on the subject of music and memory; from muscle memory in the development of performance practice; to the development and maintenance of mental health through the many ways in which music interacts with our memory while learning, performing composing or listening. Music, as an activity, it would seem, has a profound link with how we remember, personally and collectively. Whether recalling very recent personal happenings or distant historic events as they pass across our collective experienced time.

In the fabulous pages that make up his *The Time of Music*, Jonathan Kramer gives us a striking collection of approaches as to how composers and performers might adopt certain strategies to shape their canvas of time to – as it were – play games with or beguile the memory of the listener. This could be achieved within sections, movements of works or across an entire piece or even whole genres. Needless to say the musical ciphers being thrust upon this canvas of time will often be evocative of places and identities; thus transforming the memory of the listener on many different levels simultaneously.

It would also seem that the memory games that music plays upon us are also good for our survival as a species, since, as David Huron puts it so wonderfully in his *Sweet Anticipation* – …the biological purpose of expectation is to prepare an organism for the future. Remembering, anticipating and expecting is of course at the core of music listening – and is integral to the art of music composition and performance.

The importance of music upon collective memory and political stability, is perhaps most profoundly summed up in certain quarters of Plato's *Ethos theory*:

"…But such [musical] innovation should not be recommended…the music … of a country cannot be altered without major political changes – we have Damon's word for it and I believe him" – Damon of Athens, according to Plato (*Republic 424)*

Here I would like to finish my discussion with you for now. But I wonder if you be interested to listen to a piece of music or sound-art work that I composed recently: *Stations of the Clyde*. In some ways it acts also as a sonic work of psychogeograpy, it traces a journey across Glasgow that I used to take on countless occasions, from the city's 'South Side' to its 'West End.' It celebrates the accents and words uttered by passers by of all ages; echoing through places of travel, work and recreation (Glasgow Central Station, St. Enoch and Kelvingrove Subway stations, Argyle Street and Kelvingrove Park), transformed by the city's nature and climate (birdsong and drops of rain, so much beautiful rain). At times the work's rhythmic inflections mimic those of the city's discourse or of its mighty industry. All of this was to conjure various places, known, cherished and remembered by me, to capture and explore them as part of my sonic identity (irrespective of my nationality, as you know I see the place of one's birth as being in many ways a simple accident of place and time and nothing to do with personal choice).

It's dedicated to a dear friend of mine, Patricia, who is in all senses a daughter of the Clyde. I hope that you enjoy the work. Thank you so much for being a fine companion today and for listening to me so patiently and attentively.

Owen Dudley Edwards

The title of this essay is entirely imaginary and has no reference to nay living person.

It was in fact caused by *The Drouth* working itself into a diet of the postmodern heebie-jeebies or else trying to work you into them by declaring our theme word to be 'Close'.

I could, of course, have been inspired by it to go up the Close and down the stair… but that was where we came in.

Postmodern means proptermodern: to be postmodern you have to think in Latin — that's where the post came from (never mind, just yet, about where it will go to).

First past the postmodern this time is Ian Rankin who has just given birth to *Saints of the Shadow Bible*, sequel to *Standing in Another Man's Grave*, his last-year repentance for having apparently bade farewell to his hardboiled Edinburgh policeman in *Exit Lines*. He is probably the most likable and best principled author most of us are likely to meet, of an instinctive courtesy they simply don't make nowadays, but his Inspector Rebus is as tough as his latest problem. This may give publicity-obsessed witch-doctors and reviewers the basis for some bad jokes on the lang-syne-deid Embro-Glasgay rivalry but unlike reviewers and rivals Rebus and Rankin are real, if not always on the same wavelength. Rebus has achieved Parable status. We are all Rebus.

That seems to imply I think Rankin is Jesus Christ. I don't, but if on Judgement Day he turns out to be, I wouldn't be 100% surprised.

Rankin himself is a product of Edinburgh University's English Literature Department, and has himself become meat for lit. crit. with results such as Aaron Kelly's in *Masculinity in Scottish and Northern Irish Crime Fiction*:

In drawing correlations between both detective and criminal, Rankin's work also touches upon the serial killer figure which has become such a cultural obsession of late. Why is this obsession so present? Given that a British Prime Minister, Margaret Thatcher, once claimed that 'there is no such thing as society', I would offer the following explanation. We foist on to the figure of the serial killer all our anxieties about our society itself, about its dominant trends and ultimate values. If the serial killer is defined as asocial, lacking in emotional ties to others, a loner and an enigma gesturing to the social fracture of our times then we can locate the figure within the alienated individualisation of consumer capitalism. We can go further, however, when we consider that the attributes that I have just ascribed to be serial killer — asociality, lacking emotional ties to others, solitariness – are all simultaneously characteristics of the detective too. Rebus, for instance, is defined by his 'failed relationships'.

Alas, Edinburgh's leading serial killers Burke and Hare, were highly social, to their great profit.

The word 'Rebus' itself, as I recall from pre-1914 *Little Folks* bound volumes, means well-known names jumbled up. We know Rebus but can't recognise him. That is because we are him. In the words of Walt Kelly's *Pogo*, we have met the enemy, and they are us.

He may also be classical. Do we follow Horace? 'Rebus in Arduis' = 'in every crisis' (and God knows he is). Or are we programmed by Cicero? '*His Rebus Disjectis*' These thing having been chucked aside. And that is the supreme theme of this last book, of its precursor, and in a way of them all. Modern civilisation aka methods aka technology aka transparency is convinced it has no use for Rebus, and *Vice versa*, but neither can fully let go of one another.

All detective stories since 1891 are variations on Sherlock Holmes, the more so the more apparently remote. Rankin characteristically grasped that nettle (in part by making Conan Doyle the murderer in one short story). Conan Doyle, at least in the earliest Holmes stories, was thinking of Edinburgh while spinning around Holmes a city called London built up from an obsolete map of his father's. Rankin put his creation in the Edinburgh he knew and does it so well that the Edinburgh reader feels the damned thing, not to say the damned detective, closing in on every side, looking at us from mirrors, even when we close the book.

It accords with Rankin's ascetic manner and message that his method dispenses with the target of the Scottish Enlightenment's market research — London, the great wen, the great parish pump, the great provider, for whose sake Hume and Robertson purged their Scotticisms, Scott from time to time turned his into cod-medieval, Rowling stole an Edinburgh (K)Night bus and split a platform by three-quarters. How do the Londoners, citizens of the most inverted backwater on earth, cope with a best-seller openly writing about Edinburgh, a place either known as the backcloth of an epidemic of bad comedians or the suburb of Morningside (spelt Kelvinside)? And the New Yorkers (ditto, ditto, except they know it's in England)?

Rankin has in truth proclaimed independence before the rest of us, and did it long ago. In fact much of our present progress towards Independence (and whatever happens in September, it's been a progress unthinkable fifty or forty or thirty years ago.) is a progress because Rankin has conquered a vast international public and made it think Scottish, his fellow-countrymen along with them. Or at least think Edinburgh. *Standing in Another Man's Grave* gets us up towards Aberdeen and Inverness, but am I alone in finding it less real? Certainly *Saints of the Shadow Bible* has clear mastery and movement (however perplexing the puzzles) harmonising with the author's topographical music never more assured than now. Rankin may well have the firmest literary hold on Edinburgh since Stevenson.

This is not to claim that he orchestrates Edinburgh space and time simultaneously as Muriel Spark does in The *Prime of Miss Jean Brodie*. The past is crucial to S*aints of the Shadowy Bible*, but it is past revealed, admitted, assessed, questioned, faced, ducked, confronted and expiated in the present. And *Saints* is as good as it is partly because Standing surveyed, established, and cleared ground for it, self-circumscribed though the stories are. And Conan Doyle still haunts his impious disciple Rankin with results of varying quality. Rankin ended *Exit Lines* with a supposed farewell to Rebus, as Conan Doyle once took leave of Holmes in 'The Final Problem' (*Memoirs of Sherlock Holmes* (1893)), but where Holmes went offstage apparently killing himself so as to kill his archenemy Professor Moriarty, Rebus took his exit in a desperate but successful personal resuscitation of his dying supreme adversary Cafferty. (Does that name derive from Percy French's 'Phil the Fluther's Ball'?

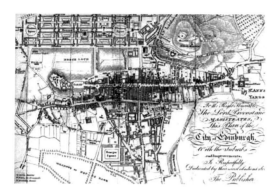

Then Phil struck up to the best of his ability,

The ladies and the gentlemen they went and
did their share.

'Begar, then, Mick, 'tis you that have agility.'
'Begar then, Mrs Cafferty, you're leppin'
like a hare!'

Joyce's *Finnegans Wake* had a similar musical origin.
Rebus's facial breathpumping dance of life to save
Cafferty is glorious ironic caricature of the Platonic
original.)

But if *Standing in Another Man's Grave* weakens
itself to pump life into its sequel, its own place as
sequel to *Exit Lines* is automatically bled in its wake.
Cafferty was never going to rival Professor Moriarty,
certainly, in part because Conan Doyle had the
genius never actually to bring Moriarty before the
reader: he is variously seen in retrospective glimpses
by one of the characters, or apparently witnessed
from a train fruitlessly gesturing on the platform,
or beheld in silhouette walking up a mountain. But
where similar attempts by other great detective-
story writers founder in comparison with 'The Final
Problem' and its sequel 'The Empty House', Rankin's
realism satisfies its modest agenda. It makes sense
that Cafferty, once recovered and at liberty should
have a drink or two with Rebus, it makes sense that
neither of them really enjoy it — theirs are not the
swashbuckling rival hostilities of Homes-and-Moriarty
duel — and it makes sense that Rebus incurs
suspicion from both fellow-cops and crooks from
these aborted civilities. But it is anti-climatic, and
ultimately Cafferty fizzles out. He was well managed
while he infected the action of various Rebus stories,
and did his modicum towards the menace as master-
crook should, but he was at best a Senior Lecturer,
never quite a Professor.

It was Conan Doyle's extraordinary achievement to
begin with Holmes stories set in the very recent past
which yet established themselves in their period and
Zeitgeist so well that they effortlessly slid into real
past and their readers moved from generation
to generation. Conan Doyle was proud of his
historical fiction, and in the Brigadier Gerard stories
produced the best series of historical short stories in
the English language, but in the Holmes cycle what
he wrote became historical fiction over the years.
Whatever Conan Doyle's shortcomings as a witness
to the past, he has won immortality as a witness
from the past. Can Rankin rival that? Well, at least he
will compel future historians to draw on his powers
of observation devouring his own times, and never
more than in *Saints of the Shadow Bible*, where he
has some very shrewd deductions to make on the
Independence fight. He has jocularly informed the
press that Rebus will vote 'No' and his more likeable
sidekick Detective Inspector Siobhan Clarke will vote
'Yes' and he doesn't know or at least won't say what
he will vote himself. None of this matters in this story,
but Rankin has reached ominous conclusions about
the abominable No-men.

Ian Rankin by now is a master craftsman, and thus
relied on by his pubic (or, as today's vulgarity likes to
say, his customers). They know they will enjoy being
teased and tricked by him, combining hardboiled
action with clever detection, which his master, Conan
Doyle, achieved in *The Valley of Fear* as Holmes,
investigating the murder of a retired hardboiled
detective, realises the supposed victim is the killer.
Indeed *Saints* turns a trick mixing *The Valley of Fear*
with Agatha Christie's *Curtain* where Poirot is the
ultimate killer: we are confronted with long ago
corrupt police crimes and modern cover-ups and
face the real possibility that Rebus may have
committed one or more of these faraway
crookeries. It is no mean achievement to make your
readers believe that your hero of many previous

quests could yet prove a one-time baddie. And he does make us believe it. But he doesn't deal in the incredible. If he plays with the Independence theme he doesn't offer a scenario in which the Prime Minister of the UK tells the Scottish people he knows they won't vote the way he wants, so he wants them to do what they are told by the previous Chancellor of the Exchequer, whom the Prime Minister publicly blames for the worst depression in UK history. That Prime Minister, in this scenario, untouched by realism or Rankin, even expresses the hope his own predecessor as Prime Minister will join the accursed ex-chancellor in telling the Scottish people to vote against independence, although those two economic architects of UK ruin no longer work together because of what one wrote about another in a book so moronic nobody could read it. Rankin doesn't even include Unionist quotation of economic astrologers crystal-gazing even more ruin as the result of Independence, despite the fact that if their powers were of any value they could have forecast the great depression. Rankin knows that not even his powers of persuasion could lead his audience to believe in fiction as foothing as that.

But Rankin does point out to us how Unionist cardsharps fix the game behind the scenes. Knighthoods and lordships will be flourished or withheld according to the prosed recipient's enmity or otherwise to Independence. Was this why Andy Murray received a mere decoration instead of the knighthood he so clearly deserved for claiming Wimbledon for Britain after a septuagenarian's lifetime? He has so far refused to declare for either side in the Referendum. You win Wimbledon's greatest trophy, you even win Wimbledon in the London Olympic games but the UK government like any fairground conman rates it close — but no cigar. If the present government did any work when getting drunk at the taxpayers' expense in its Oxbridge years, it could have studied the enactment of the Union in 1707 which created the state of Britain, and that of 1800 which abolished Britain (to make the United Kingdom of Great Britain and Ireland), and read of the 'honours' bestowed on converts to Union in those years specifically gaudy peerages whose inheritors still adorn the scandal-sheets. And if they didn't learn it for themselves, they have innumerable intellectual lickspittles to do it for them, once again at the expense of the UK taxpayer.

Rankin makes his chief No-Man a corrupt cop of old times, whose judicious resignation under pressure then freed him up to accumulate millions in 'business'. His cop corruption has included framing a barman whom he found insufficiently deferential. But squeaky-clean cops still in full service may find promotional and patronage reasons to bully their subordinates into the 'No' ranks —

> Rebus knew his boss's feelings on the topic — like Everyone else in the office, he'd had his ear bent by Page about the need for Scotland to remain part of the UK.

And here the cops in general become all of us, harmonising with Rebus as Everyman (he is too old and too barnacled to think of himself as Everyperson). Who knows how many hundreds of thousands of Scottish wage-slaves are subject until September to cruder and subtler forms of employer blackmail against Independence? Saki's 'A Young Turkish Catastrophe' (1909) tells of an election for which women get the vote and a polygamist reactionary is then elected having declared to his wives 'that every vote given to his opponent meant another sack thrown into the Bosporus!' No-men have little to learn from him when it comes to lack of scruple. Casual punters may have little to fear from the former Chancellor of the Exchequer announcing that in the event of Independence there shall be signs in the sun, and in the moon, and in the stars, and upon the earth distress of nations, with perplexity: the sea and the waves roaring: Men's hearts failing them for fear, and for looking after those things which are coming on the earth: for the powers of heaven shall be shaken. We may laugh these forecasts from the No-men to scorn, but should this be preliminary to 'And therefore unless Scotland votes No, you lose your job'. Where are you then? Before devolution, Sir Bruce Pattullo was fool enough to play that game in the open, sincerely believing as he did that no other answer was possible but 'Yes, Sir Bruce.' His Bank of Scotland customers gave him other answers and within months his resignation was written for him. Not so now. Bankers have learned camouflage. And we have learned enough about bankers to make Sir Bruce sound like Truthful James, however dim in other respects. Nobody work this more than the No-men, loudly as they prate that we must reward any bankers who swindle us for fear they might swindle someone else in preference to us and thus diminish the Glory of the Union.

People who talk about ticking the boxes live mentally in boxes for ticks. Rankin like the rest of us has limits to originality but in dealing with persons or bodies thinking only in clichés (which usually means not thinking at all), he knows how to send the boxes home to roost. Knighthoods are inevitably festooned into the commerce of 'no'. And Rankin makes an interesting point of sincerity:

> 'You know I'm right, don't you?' she asked quietly.
> 'I think you knew it then too. Saunders had to have

something on Stefan Gilmour. When you saw Gilmour the other night, how was he? When Blantyre told him about reopening the case, how did he react?'

   'He was fine; he acted fine.'

'Maybe acting is one of those thing he does well. Have you seen him on TV, campaigning for Scotland to stay in the union?'

   'I doubt that's an act.'
   'But it's a role he's playing.'

   Dryden's 'Absalom and Achitophel' has some analogy.

Then, seiz'd with Fear, yet still affecting Fame,
Usurp'd a Patriot's All-atoning Name.

The Fear in the Independence struggle may include the obvious fear of loss of parliamentary seats, jobs, patronage, power, influence, &c, &c. Rankin is right to remind us that it may include Fear of exposure for past ill-doing, especially since in the case of most defenders of the Union they are also defending their complicity in bringing the UK into illegal wars. Because personal profit and private speculation lend sincerity to Unionist crusades, we should be able to diagnose where the role is adopted without question

but yet is hardly felt in the marrow of the bones. In the devolution struggle of the 1970s there were many role-players: but there were also bone-marrow No-men such as Tam Dalyell and Allan Campbell McLean. It's hard to find them today. The Tory party is suspected of yearning for Scottish independence in hopes of future Tory election majorities; Labour says 'No' to get jobs for its No-men and if also for justice, seems to have lost the language in which to record the fact; the Liberal Democrats seem no different. Above all the Unionist repetition of clichés, the Mumbo-Jumbo in which to hoodoo Scots, seems afraid of thought above all. 'Be-eht-er To-geh-eh-ther' sloganizes itself to drown all debate in the approved fashion of *Animal Farm's* sheep — ' Four Legs Good, Two Legs Bad' until the day comes to affirm 'Four Legs Good, Two Legs Be-eht-er'.

And Fear may have other relevance. So far the defence of the Union has been along predictable lines, used-up politicians spouting patriotism, reliance on the superstition engendered by advertisement. The balance of polls keeps the Union bright. But if the margin between 'Yes' and 'No' seems to narrow, as it may be doing now, we may find ourselves in a much bloodier war. Rebus at one point remarks that 'politics in Scotland has never been so ugly'. Pray God this is not a Voice from the Future. And in the process, will we ever get an honest expression of opinion as to whether Scotland should be independent or not? Stephen Maxwell's invaluable *Arguing for Independence* ends with a series of comprehensive answers to questions beginning 'Aye, but'. Aye but beneath these rational expositions breathes there an electorate with soul so dead that it really wants independence while being afraid to admit it to pollsters, to employers, to any potentially more authoritative questioner? Professor John Curtice is a pleasure to observe psephologising, notably because of his demeanour of an unconceited sparrow who has killed Cock Robin but would never boast about it. And his favourite cliché, 'In Truth', has a near-metaphysical air, in contrast to the tedium of other people's 'At the End of the Day', 'When all has been Said and Done', or 'In the last analysis (my own one, unless I catch myself doing it). But where is the Truth we are supposed to be in, other than an attempt from Pontius Pilate to be funny while deciding which prisoners to crucify and which to flog to death? Will most Labour supporters in Scotland vote 'No' from loyalty to their London-loving leaders while secretly refusing to admit to themselves they want an Independent Scotland? Will prominent former leaders of the SNP really hope for a 'no' vote rather than let Alex Salmond have the glory of success? Certainly Alex Salmond himself knows that danger, as he signalled by putting Nicola Sturgeon at the head of the SNP 'Yes' forces where — in truth — she is making converts previously repelled by him.

The Truth (occasionally synonymous with *The Drouth*) made a startling incursion on Scottish politics the other day, and its presence threw its far more frequent absence into ugly relief. The Chamber of Deputies in Holyrood was debating Same-Sex Marriage initially with heterosexual civilities, but then came the real thing. Ruth Davidson, leader of the Tory Party in Scotland, began her speech she acknowledged as probably the most important she would ever make. Her situation had its ironies. She did not say it, but she was speaking for the Bill whither most of her followers declined to follow her, and she clearly would have spoken for it had she been the only Tory voting for it. She is an agreeable colleague, fencing like a precocious D'Artagnan with some hope of a musketeer's commission some day, but never quite able to shake off the conceit of word-perfection in whatever line London may be cooking up for their hapless Holyrood hoplites. As it happens London is also for same sex but much more obviously mutinying in the rear (so to speak). But on this day Ruth Davidson would lead and be led by nobody but herself, and if she resembled Joan of

Arc in thereby exhilarating followers that was for them to show. One could see the touch of regret as she thrilled in being herself, for this one time flying her own flag, answering her own physiology. She will be adroit, adept, able as she pirouettes for the Union, of course, but she will never defend it with the blazing sincerity with which she demanded the right to love and be loved as equal with the love that had brought her into the world and gave her so happy a childhood. In truth, she must surely scent the richness of the destiny awaiting her if Scotland does become Independent. What a leader she could be then! But she is forced to campaign to retain the status of David Cameron's little drummer girl.

Downing Street's message-girl she must remain, but at least it gave her priority to give the first gay speech that day, and she was followed by fine work from several others in similar case. To me there was a great thrill in hearing Jim Eadie, Marco Biagi, and several other SNP MSPs speak for themselves and their gay identities, I having joined the party in 1974 when any such proclamation would have been unthinkable. Or if thinkable, about as likely as the majority of Scots in 1974 voting for independence. Gay liberation officially began in 1971 but it took a long time to infect societies such as ours, with a far longer one to get legislative acceptance of the right of two human beings to love one another and be honoured as such. The final phase of the struggle was not so much in Parliament, important as that *Te Deum* was, but in the streets and in the churches. And the latter involved some major tragedies, above all that of Cardinal Keith Patrick O'Brien, whose work for ecumenism, for environment and against weapons of mass destruction far outweighed any wrong he did. But in almost a magical reversal of roles, on gay identities it was the Lesbians and male homosexuals who told the truth, and the clergy, official guardians of truth, who were concealing it. The teaching of Jesus was formidably apposite: those with beams in their own eye had no right to denounce supposed motes in the eyes of their brothers and sisters. The phrase 'unfit for purpose' has been bandied about the Roman Catholic hierarchy in Scotland. This is unreasonable, since we are all unfit for God's purposes and have to do the best we can. But the magisterium of the Roman Catholic church is in no position to teach faith and morals in relation to homosexual love, steeped as so many of its princes apparently are, in convert expressions of homosexual lust. The Catholic faithful may now be in serious doubt as to how much of their faith is held by those who officially lead it. The relevance of this to Protestant and all other clergy will be obvious.

It alters the lighting on literature no less than history, notably on such figures as the Welsh short-story writer, novelist crypto-gay Rhys Davies (1901–78) whose biography by the Welsh cultural encyclopaedist Meic Stephens (Parthian) is a masterly monument for those who love the rich Welsh tonality of Davies's work, and a sensitive introduction for those still to make that great discovery. Stephens's own biographical note on the dust-jacket concludes some-what pointedly that 'He has four children and ten grandchildren, all Welsh-speaking, and lives with his wife Ruth in Cardiff' a reasonable insurance for the historian of a gay author apparently as promiscuous as Joe Orton or Tennessee Williams.

Davies's work certainly takes on a new meaning when we realise that he may never have had sexual relations with a woman, and that many of his female characters were the supreme point of author identification with his creations. But he won impressive readerships the overwhelming majority of which must have taken him to be straight, insofar as they thought about it all. Those of his reviewers who were themselves homosexual may have suspected his orientation: for instance the Irish Lesbian novelist Kate O'Brien, reviewing his *Under the Rose* (later staged as *No Escape*) in the *Spectator* for 4 October 1940 warmed to him.

> Mr Davies' work is new to me, and this first encounter has given me much pleasure. He draws character with an ease which suggests full reserves of novelistic power; his pages are suffused with local atmosphere that is vivid and moving, and he uses the beautiful Anglo-Welsh dialect persua- sively. He tells a violent, primitive story out of a serious conviction which sustains uneasiness in the reader's breast. The book, in fact, is full of serious talent imperfectly managed; … I have only gratitude to record for a book which took my mind refreshingly away during many hours from actual, international furies to those, more satisfactorily purging, of the imagination and the individual.

This (in truth) was writing and reviewing through the Blitz. But the hidden battleground had been bitterly disputed up to notably in the prosecution and censorship of Radclyffe Hall's *The Well of Loneliness* in 1928, in the UK, followed by its banning by the Irish Censorship Board which from 1931 to 1949 banned eleven Rhys Davies titles including *Under the Rose*. Kate O'Brien had been banned herself and in 1941 her *The Land of Spices* was banned promptly on its appearance almost certainly from its homosexual content, which consisted of one line 'She saw *Etienne* and her father in the embrace of love'. It shows the trauma of such a discovery by a hitherto protected girl, and how well

a homosexual writer can depict revulsion from such an experience. But whether showing desire or disdain, no work with evident homosexual allusion could escape the Irish Censorship Board some of whom may have needed little further instruction on the topic. They could be relied on to sniff it out from converts or closets, probably quite as clearly as Kate O'Brien when diagnosing Davies's literary potential. In the UK the Blitz may have left homosexual lifestyles less persecuted. It's a little difficult to arrest men in public lavatories when a present from Hitler may be about to award both of you a capital sentence. Alas it made the gay world all the less prepared for the vicious crackdown by the Tory government of the 1950s, including imprisonment of one of Davie's gay friends and possible lovers, Rupert Croft-Cooke, after which Davies was more secretive than ever. Is his achievement more or less when one knows his thinking and his writing may have seen the same story with different genders? Stephens leaves our imaginations to explore such clues as an otherwise unidentified photograph inscribed 'Kind regards, Roy' showing one of the Welsh Guards in 1938 (Roy may not have been the guardsman and since the illustration is subtitled 'Postcard' probably was not, but merely reflected a common interest uniting Roy and Davies). The more we ponder it, the more the Fairy' Queen's yearning for the Guardsman in Iolanthe can never be the same again.

Stephens naturally is at his best contextualising Davies's Welshness more precisely than his gaiety. But Davies's place in the hidden gay perspectives of his critics is worthy of pursuit. Stephens himself has been invaluable to the mass readership Davies still deserves whether in getting a corpus of the short stories into recent print, or in assembling an instructive if over-theoretical bouquet of essays by (some very) divers hands *Decoding the Hare* (2001). Any biographer of a literary figure who has played with autography knows that there lies (in how many senses?) his major antagonist, and Stephens ably confronts Davies's from the outset:

> The enigmatic title of the 'autobiographical beginning', *Print of a Hare's Foot*, a most unreliable book from start to finish in that it often fails to tally with the known facts and disguises people and events with adroit use of smoke and mirrors, is in fact a reference to its author's own ambiguous sexual nature. It conceals much more than it reveals.

And he delves far and wide as to what it might mean, convincingly for the most part. But Davies whether lying or flying can always be made to yield more. His friendship with D.H. Lawrence rightly wins a chapter here, but one that might have recalled words from Lawrence's *Women in Love*, rather a closet gay text itself:

> 'You yourself, don't you find it a beautiful clean thought, a world empty of people, just uninterrupted grass, and a hare sitting up.'

Michael Innes would use that for an epigraph accentuating the title for his thriller *Hare Sitting Up* (1959). Stephens tells us Davies liked murder stories and the book or at least the title would hardly have eluded him: *Print from a Hare's Foot* appeared in 1969. It would be nice to think he had a happy loving relationship with Roy or someone else, guarded or unguarded, but however close one or two such encounters may have been, there seems little trace of cigar-ash. Stephens notes a number of unfulfilled hopes for lovers who would prove heterosexual, through it is less certain than he thinks that all of these would have rejected at least one night however much they would decline a thousand. Davies's portrayals of human relationships in his own native Wales do not deny emotion, and indeed are almost faultless in their measurement, but the clear hand and eye record at best empathetically, seldom if ever sympathetically Davies does not mock his fellow-Welsh, but he shows their readiness to mock themselves. One might call his kinder and certainly a more accurate eye than Dylan Thomas's, and compared with Davies's best Welsh work *Under Mild Wood* may momentarily seem childish, yet Thomas is less afraid to show love of his land while sending it up rotten. Davies can bring to his fiction the science of Alexander Pope, where Thomas holds the sublimity as well as the stupidity of Shelley.

The book therefore that seems yet needful for the devoted Meic Stephens to give us on Davies would be one on the lines of the Routledge 'Critical Heritage' series, anthologising texts or at least excerpts from the literary judgements on individual writers passed in print or in correspondence or conversation by their contemporaries. We could form better judgements by confronting his critics gay and straight (or mixed) as well as by awareness of his own occasional forays in reviewing or sponsoring. It may have been that he was less balanced, or perhaps less honest, in noticing gay authors. Stephens (p263) declares that Davies 'dismissed Angus Wilson, who dealt with homosexual themes in a coded way, just as Davies did, as 'England's leading specialist in bitchery'. This says little for Davies's critical powers, unless Stephens has foisted

his own misreading on his biographical subject. Wilson's *Hemlock and After* (1951) was the first major novel in English to deal openly and sympathetically with homosexual themes as its main plot. Davies's comment may be justified if taken straight: the novel captures gay bitchery neatly enough, though much more concerned with gay self-respect and dignity. But Davies's judgement could have been the product of shame: Wilson had won far more celebrity as a novelist and won it for a courage Davies had avoided.

Stephens while redolent with valuable information needs care with these critical contemporaries. He tells us that while Davies 'allowed' Geoffrey West to read several of his novels in typescript' ('allowed' is good since Davies urgently needed favourable criticism and West had reviewed him for the *Times Literary Supplement*), their 'friendship' ended when West 'expressed a critical opinion of *The Red Hills*, suggesting that its main characters were seen in isolation "in hillside detachment", from their environment citing West's review of the book which he dates in the TLS (15 December 1936). *The Red Hills* and its reviews had actually appeared in 1932, and West, author of monographs on Charles Darwin and Arnold Bennett was still applauding Davies on 31 July 1937 in *Time and Tide* for his *My Wales* (A.G. Macdonnell, author of the hilarious *England, Their England*, wrote *My Scotland* for the same (Jarrold) series). His judgement of Davies of Wales there seems as good as any:

> …the same level vision prevails, the sense of writing about something real and positive, whose virtues are strong enough to stand without demanding suppression of its faults. It is hard to express the spirit of a book in a sentence, but somewhere here Mr Davies speaks of those poets who can 'capture the elusive Welsh soul and, like a wet eel wrapped in a piece of newspaper, clothe it in words'. *My Wales* is really for those who can appreciate how in that fresh, unexpected simile he combines at once a gibe, a laugh, and an affectionate salute.

The great V.S. Pritchett, for a quarter-century leading book critic of the *New Statesman*, similarly told its readers on 13 March 1937 of Davies's *A Time to Laugh*:

> …the material is excellent, in the first place because the Welsh are a nation of toughs, roughs and poetic humbugs, vivid in their speech, impulsive in behaviour and riddled with a sly and belligerent tribalism. Mr Rhys Davies handles this expertly. He is passionate, athletic comical and

lyrical by turns. He is out in the streets when the windows smash.

One passage in *My Wales* cut startlingly deep:

Harder times came. As coal prices perversely and fiendishly wallowed in the doldrums, disregarding these miners who could hardly afford a lump of soap for their black backs, the owners would give notice of a 5 or 10 per cent reduction on that Sliding Scale which already the miners were fuming against. This was in the early 'nineties. In London, Oscar Wilde was elegantly sauntering down the Haymarket dropping jewels of wit about Art for Art's sake, though by this time there was only the ghost of a carnation in his hand. He too, was preaching revolt and was of similar texture to the coal-miners, intrinsically. Carnation and coal-pick, art-revolt and labour agitations, gay and hard nineties! The old century was not going to be allowed to die as smugly and complacently as its apparent success warranted.

If Davies would not make it easy to fit him into gay literature, he opened up a major seam in gay history. Davies was for many readers the voice of Wales in the 1930s and 1940s (Dylan Thomas, aided by his own apocalyptic death, captured the 1950s). George Orwell in the *Manchester Evening News* for 18 October 1945 hailed Davies as one of the 'small handfuls of successful short story writers in England at this moment' while isolating the genre's current difficulty 'of producing something which is a real story with action and development in it, and which at the same time is readable and has a clear connection with real life'/ the Wales he found in Davies was 'grotesque … nearer to Hans Anderson than to Maupassant'. Reviewing Davies's *Selected Stories* he itemised:

The first deals with a corpse who comes to life just before being buried, to the dismay of her sisters, who have spent a lot of money on the funeral.

The second deals with the refusal of some old women in an alms-house to use a newly-installed water closet.

The third deals with a young miner who has never seen his wife with her clothes off.

The fourth describes a Welsh family squabbling over their father's belongings while he lies dying upstairs.

The fifth deals with an eccentric old maid who insists on talking her cow to church with her.

The sixth describes an insurance agent whose home life temporarily improves because he is getting

tenderer meat for his meals, which is really due to the fact that his wife is having an affair with the butcher.

The seventh deals with a dwarf with a gift for drawing who rapes and murders a girl who has treated him in a heartless way.

The eighth deals with a fatuous poet whose wife ends by chopping up for firewood the oak throne he has won at an Eisteddfod.

Orwell regarded this as 'sacrificing credibility', 'improbable', 'abnormal'. He clearly enjoyed it in preference to the norm in contemporary short stories which he summed up as 'A lonely woman sits in her maisonette waiting for the telephone to ring: it doesn't ring'. But this falls under the Orwellian norm, that if we are enjoying something it must, in some way, be wrong. This survives perhaps from Orwell's Englishness, which at that time meant a superior form of sophistication. It was not only their common homosexuality (they even shared living quarters for a time) which Scotland's pre-eminent short story writer Fred Urquhart, significantly anthologised in the same 'Hour-glass Library' series by the Dublin Jewish publisher Maurice Fridberg. Frank O'Connor was its Irish offering both in another *Selected Stories* and in his translation from Irish-Gaelic bawdy epic verse by Brian Merriman *The Midnight Court* (banned by the Irish Censorship Board in English though not, or course, in Irish). Davies would have reached an Irish audience with much less Orwellian alienation. The Irish novelist Liam O'Flaherty thought Davies's early story 'A Bed of Feathers' 'one of the finest things written since the war', presumably all the more readily because its theme, a young man's love for his aged half-brother's wife touched similar notes to Synge's *In the Shadow of the Glen*, T.C. Murray's *Autumn Fire*, Eugene O'Neill's *Desire Under The Elms*, and the old Celtic Legends of Deirdre, Gràinne, Isolde, as well as the Greek Hippolytus (Euripides) and its descendent Racine's Phedre. *Shadows of the Glen* also stars the unwelcome resurrection. In its extreme form (Deirdre, Gràinne, isolde, Hippolytus and Rhys Davies the aged lustful patriarch kills the young rival.

But all of this likens creative artists from countries of recent Celtic speech. O'Flaherty was born with Gaelic as his first language on the Galway Aran Islands. Davies is never known to have spoken a word of Welsh, widely though it was and is still spoken in other parts of Wales than his. Here the Irish (and, as we shall see, Scottish) link is with Anglophones apparently ignorant of the non-English tongues spoken by so many of their fellow countrymen, and the question of what they made of the native language they did not speak. Jonathan Swift for Ireland and Walter Scott for Scotland are two major if (on this) somewhat undervalued examples. Their own connection is strong, if neglected. Scott wrote a life of Swift, when editing his works in 19 volumes, which he began in 1808 and published in 1814. He published his first novel *Waverley*, anonymously, the year he finished Swift. A massive investigation of Scott's use of Swift in creative writing is needed, but one point may be easily deduced. Scott's novels were obviously influenced by *Gulliver's Travels*, the first one describing the experiences of an Englishman cast away in a strange land whose inhabitants were Scots rather than pygmies or giants. He plays variants of the device in *Rob Roy* and several other novels, reversing its course and gender in *The Heart of Midlothian*. Before tackling Swift and all his works Scott had faced his own problems in needing to comprehend a Scotland whose language for most of its territory he did not speak. While writing in a language — English — which he spoke seldom. Laying down the law about the culture of languages unknown to us seems to be more frequent than we may imagine: the late High Trevor-Roper pronounced that Irish Gaelic poetry was much superior to Scots-Gaelic while knowing neither language and confusing the findings of his main source which he thought described status of poets in 1700 and in reality was discussing those in 600. That he should have been taken seriously by English scholars reminds us of the frailty of Anglo-Scots mutual understanding, absurd as are the English credulity and the Scots failure to see the English capacity for credulity. Significantly these follies were engendered by Trevor-Roper's attempts to discuss what he regarded as James MacPherson's frauds in Scottish Gaelic literature. The contrast dividing them is this: eighteenth-century Macpherson's frauds were based on his own monumental scholarship, twentieth-century Trevor-Roper's on empty academic pontifications. Macphersons represented himself as having translated Gaelic epics: in fact he had built imaginatively if puritanically on anti-heroic poems and folk-stories still recoverable from Scots and Irish Gaelic-speakers in Argyll, the isles, north Antrm,

anodyned – not to say emasculated – the complex and sometimes contradictory characters of the heroes as a result of which dry-cleaning they became appropriate exemplars enjoying Napoleon's approval.

Scott summed up what are still recognised today as the realities when commencing his discussion of the topic in reviewing the Highland Society's *Report ...[on] the Poems of Ossian* and Malcolm Laing's anti-Macpherson edition (Sarcastically entitled *The Poems of Ossian, &c., containing the Poetical Works of James Macpherson, Esquire, in Prose and Rhyme*) Scott himself writing in the Edinburgh Review for July 1805:

> It is allowed, on all hands, that numberless traditions were current in Ireland, concerning the Fenij or Fions, a species of militia inhabiting Leinster, and commanded by Fin MacCoul, termed by Macpherson, Fingal, the son of Comhal. Among these warriors, we recognize the well known names of Gall Mac-Morn, (Gaul, the son of Morni), of Osgur the son of Oisin, the Ossian of Macpherson, of Fergus and Fillan, and other warriors; and, finally, of Ossian or Oisin himself, who lived, like Aneurin, to 'weep and sing the fall' of his deceased friends. Aneurin composed his *Y Gododdin* about 600 A.D. in the future Edinburgh (or at least Lothians) in what was than it's prevailing language, Welsh (or, you prefer, Old Briton), and Scott's use of it as parallel showed more understanding of comparative Celtic studies than most commentators over the last two and half centuries. The image of Oisin lamenting his deceased family and friends having survived by magic long after their deaths, remained proverbial in Gaelic and was being used in late twentieth-century political commentary. For all that he became known as the American Scott, James Fenimore Cooper's book-title *The Last of the Mohicans* came to have the same meaning as Oisin surviving the Fianna, and he himself derived his native American material in part from Macpherson's as well as Scott's Highlanders (particularly from Rob Roy). The acknowledgement of primarily Irish origin for what Macpherson had sought to make Scottish heroic sagas with derisive dismissal of Irish claims was characteristic realism from Scott: in fact a thousand years ago western Scotland, the Hebrides, and northern Ireland were culturally unified by a maritime people leaving common folklore.

Scott's generosity of mind dictated his conclusion saluting Macpherson:

But, while we are compelled to renounce the pleasing idea, 'that Fingal lived, and that Ossian sang', our national vanity may be equally flattered by the fact, that a remote, and almost a barbarous corner of Scotland, produced, in the 18th century, a bard capable not only of making an enthusiastic impression on every mind susceptible of poetic beauty, but of giving a new tone to poetry throughout all Europe.

As to the new tone in poetry, if anyone sought a monument they could look at him, author of *The Lay of the Last Minstrel,* published that year and with its narrator poet as ancient survivor admirably reworked from Ossian. But Scott's interest in Ossian had begun deep in the eighteen century perhaps in the earliest 'teens, such as in January 1783 when the *Gentleman's Magazine* actually printed in parallel Gaelic and English texts a verse dialogue/disputation between Ossian and St Patrick as recited by a blacksmith called Mac-Nab in Dalmaly. Despite the centuries dividing their birthdates many Gaelic poems and other tales claimed to record Ossian-and-Patrick duets, usually on the assumption that Ossian/Oisin had lived for what he had thought a brief interval in the Land of Youth, *Tir na n-Og*, but that on his return to Ireland it proved 300 years' duration. The initial note in such verses was one of disputation between the virtues of the pagan Fianna and Christianity, and the *Gentleman's Magazine* was certainly true to that tradition:

OSSIAN:
O Clerk that singest the Psalms! I think thy notions are rude;
That thou wilt not hear my songs, of the heroes of Fingal [correctly, 'of the Fianna' or, as Scott would say, Fions'],
Whom thou has never seen.

CLERK:
I find thy greatest delight is in relating the stories of the actions of Fingal and his heroes; but the sound of the Psalms is sweeter between my lips than the songs of Fingal.

OSSIAN:
If thou darest to compare thy Psalms to the old heroes of Ireland (Erin) with their drawn weapons, Clerk! I am much of opinion, I should be sorely vexed if I did not sever thy head from thy body.

CLERK:
That is in thy mercy; great Sir! The expressions of thy lips are very sweet to me. Let us rear the altar of Fingal; I would think it sweet to hear of the heroes of Fingal.

Surviving Gaelic verse from the eleventh century and beyond frequently included ruder exchanges with Ossian's bitter complaints as to Patrick's insistence of fasting and temperance contrasting with the orgies of hospitality he remembered from his father's table. The whole idea of dispute between successive historical eras naturally interested Scott, and he made it key to The Last Minstrel, using interstices between the successive six Cantos, in which the audience comment sceptically on the Minstrel's potential for surviving prowess, given his antiquity, but when they declare he would be better off seeking patronage by taking out residence in England, he burns in furious rage to:

Breathes there the man, with souls so dead,
Who never to himself hath said,
This is my own, native land!
Whose heart hath ne'er within him burned,
As home his footsteps he hath turned,
From wandering on a foreign strand! —
If such there breathe, go, mark him well;
For him so minstrel raptures swell;
High though his titles, proud his name,
Boundless his wealth as wish can claim;
Despite those titles, power, and pelf,
The wretch, concentred all in self,
Living, shall forfeit fair renown,
And, doubly dying, shall go down
To the wile dust, from whence he sprung,
Unwept, unhonoured, and unsung.

(The last word should emerge in a thunderous roar.) Did Scott ever produce a note more sublime? It is richer in being inspired by Ossian's loss of his own country not in space but in time. That form of
Patriotism is all the greater because the fatherland buried forever in the ancient time can never be recovered wherever devoted footsteps may turn, save in Ossian's attempts to recall it in lament, or saga, or lyric — – or save as in what lay ahead for Scott, the recovery of lost Scotland by literature. Scott went on to mock the mockery of pre-Macpherson poems in The Antiquary (1806) when the excessively Enlightened Jonathan Oldbuck of Monkbarns enquires about them, from a Gaelic-speaking if self-righteous nephew, Major Hector McIntyre, culminating in:

'Then', said McIntyre, 'this is the answer of Ossian:
Dare you compare your pasalms,
You son of a —'

'Son of a what!' exclaimed Oldbuck.
'It mean, I think', said the young soldier,
with some reluctance, 'son of a female dog:

Do you compare your psalms
To the tales of the bare-arm'd Fenians?'

'Are you sure you are translating that last epithet correctly, Hector?'
'Quite sure, sir', answered Hector doggedly.
'Because I should have thought the nudity might have been quoted as existing in a different part of the body.'

Douglas Hyde, founder of the Gaelic League, supreme revivalist of the Irish language, and future President of Eire, said of this in The Story of Early Gaelic Literature (1910): 'We all remember the inimitable felicity with which that great English-speaking Gael, Sir Walter Scott, has caught this Ossianic tone in the lines with which Hector McIntyre repeats for the Antiquary'. This is a fair benediction — and a reminder that the Irish revival began with a far better sense of humour than it continued under state official auspices. It also shows Scott as getting closer to the main spirit of the Ossian-Patrick poems than did either Macpherson or the Gentleman's Magazine.

Thus fared Scott with the Gaelic he did not know. Between his review of the Ossianic, and his parody of its concealed sources, lay his editorship of Swift. Did he realise that Gaelic's place in his own literary take-off with the Last Minstrel echoed Swift's with Gulliver's Travels? Professor Leo Damrosch, of Harvard, challenges existing Swift scholarship with his Jonathan Swift : His Life and His World (Yale University Press) and starts with some effective questions. Swift's love for Stella and his apparent taboo against marrying her(unless, as Walter Scott believed, he did not marry her) remain one of the great unsolved riddles of his great life, and it cannot be folded away like an Arab tent as pursuit of irrelevant smut beloved by modern biographers and even more their agents and publishers. The Journal to Stella is a great work of literature, and if we want to see it whole we should know the real relationship of the author and chief recipient. And if Swift's parentage was not what it has been commonly taken to be, it makes a great deal of difference, especially if he knew or suspected that. His most famous work Gulliver's Travels ends on what has sometimes been taken as a hatred of the human race, and self-doubts particularly on ancestry and identity could have much to do with that, especially since Gulliver's yearning not to be classified with the debased human Yahoos could easily be in part a product of Swift's self doubts of

legitimacy, where bastardy might claim superior ancestry or might derive from deeper shame. The ancestry question has been urged at times past, the Irish playwright and memorialist Denis Johnston having laboured long and impressively resulting in his *In Search of Swift* (1959) denying that Jonathan Swift senior was Swift's father on the ground that he died more than nine months before his supposed son's birth, and concluding that Swift and Stella were related through the Temple family, closely enough to prohibit their marriage under Anglican church law, to which Swift as a clergyman was necessarily obedient. Professor Damrosch points out that the leading academic biographers and commentators have flatly ignored these and other matters apparently on the unspoken assumption that no hypothesis may be considered unless it arrives clad in a doctorate of philosophy. Here at last is an academic who knows that humans may be capable of thought outside of academe. He considers Johnston's ideas, concludes there isn't sufficient evidence to make more than theories but insists we must bear their possibility in mind. His book is thus in general a new departure in common sense. Up to now it would seem the leading academic scholars on Swift regarded all

non-academic Swift studies as the work of Yahoos. The spiritual book-burning extended to Michael Foot's masterpiece *The Pen and the Sword* (1957), in which he used his own experience as a polemical journalist to show how Swift was able to bring down the Captain-General Duke of Marlborough and end Britain's part in the slaughterhouse known to history as the War of the Spanish Succession. Foot showed what history could mean when it was alive: academics, especially lit. crit. ones, apparently demand it dead. Damrosch should have made use of him having rebelled so constructively from snob college protection rackets over Swift's birth. But overall this is a truly welcome book however deplorable its necessity. Within their own sanitoria the lit. crit. lads and lassies have their own fun, the Grand Panjandrum of present-day Professors of Swiftiana, Professor Claude Rawson late of Warwick, now of Yale, despoiling rainforests to hint that however satirical Swift might have intended to be, he has to taken as meaning what he was satirising, which puts him in favour of horses above humans and wanting Protestants to eat Catholic babies. Damrosch on Swift's *Modest Proposal* is a fount of gentle sanity.

Damrosch quotes Professor Rawson on the Super-horses, the Houynhnhnms who in Rawsonian definition become 'not a statement of what man ought to be so much as a statement of what he is not': it is unclear whether Damrosch quotes this himself for satirical or for insurance purposes.

Gulliver's Travels has at least as many layers with which to stimulate our intellects as *Finnegans Wake*, but one is certainly autobiographical, the fear of English people in Ireland that the English in England will dismiss them as Irish. Brendan Behan's definition of an Anglo-Irishman — 'a Protestant on a horse' — is relevant here, as is the anti-Catholic penal law enacted by the Irish Parliament in Swift's time that if any Catholic had a horse worth more than £5 any Protestant might take it from him for £5. (Hence Conor Cruise O'Brien on duty as press officer in the Irish Department of External Affairs about 1947 being informed that a journalist has arrived: 'Mr O'Brien, the Irish Catholic is here', Conor promptly answering 'Offer him £5 for his horse'.) The notion of a Houyhnhnm is anything but flattering to the English, or to the Irish who sought to be taken for them. Damrosch is conscious of the larger questioning of humanity in the story, and rightly so, notably in its (highly religious) rebuke for human pride and

arrogance at humanity's own supposed superiority. Perhaps like his fellow-academics he is not always as alive to Swift's sense of humour as he might be: Dr Philip Roberts once defined reading *Gulliver* as walking through a garden crossed and recrossed by invisible electric fences spanning inviting landscape , and that seems an excellent maxim for all of us as we read and re-read it, unless we have the intelligence to be children and read it without remembering anything at all.

Professor Damrosch doesn't go into the question of Ireland's contribution to the origins of Gulliver. He does quote Dr Johnson's famous 'When once you have thought of big men and little men, it is very easy to do all the rest'. 'Nothing', insists Damrosch 'could be further from the truth' and this like so many of his conclusions seem fair enough, close in fact but no cigar. (Gulliver could have hoped that the Houynhnhnm might think of him as close, if ineligible for the cigar, as evidenced by their 'Farewell, gentle Yahoo' once they have evicted him, and it certainly was nice of them since a gentle Yahoo was clearly a contradiction in terms.) Swift probably did not think of the big men and little men. He was, after all, living, however reluctantly, in the land of the leprechaun which for all its kitsch has a considerable folklore antecedent, some of it found in ancient manuscript. One such case is the death of Feargus MacLeide which is prefaced by the story of little people living near that great king, unknown to him or he and his fellow–humans to them. Eventually they become known to each other with various results, some whose incredibility is matched by their obscenity, as when the queen of the little people is sexually penetrated by King Feargus for all the differences in their measurements roughly in ration to 1:12. There is even a court dwarf half Feargus' size who visits the little people. We have no proof that Swift heard a version of this story, and he is frequently taken to have been ignorant of Gaelic. But he travelled in Gaelic speaking places, and befriended Gaelic speakers and even tried a little translation of Gaelic into English verse. His insistence on reading what he wrote to servants is usually assumed to be proof of anxiety to be clear to the meanest intellect: it may have been a more scholarly activity, viz. checking at source. He was in fact a *very* Irish Anglo-Irishman. His poems make more sense when read in a Dublin accent, and not a snobbish one.

Gulliver was ultimately translated into Gaelic, long after a (very) emasculated text of the Feargus MacLeide story had been prepared for the use of schools by Canon Peter O'Leary. That was called Eisirt but the Gaelic translation of *Gulliver* was entitled Eachtrai an *Ghiolla Mhoir* (1937). Translating the title back, it means 'Adventures of the Big Servant'. Which made perfect sense in context of Gulliver in Lilliput. But it also supplies the origin of Gulliver as a name. When used in the genitive, the 'M' of 'Mor' becomes aspirate, being replaced with a 'v' sound. 'It may be that Swift picked up the name on his way from Chester', opines Damrosch, 'since he passed through a town whose innkeeper was Samuel Gulliver.' And it may not.

COMING SOON

ISSUE 48: SYSTEM

AN AUTEUR IN THE BEEB:
WAS FINLAY J. MACDONALD
THE GAELIC GRIERSON?

REGENERATION,
THE COMMON WEAL
AND OTHER GAMES

KOVESI ON KELMAN

GEOGHEGAN ON CATALONIA

Thanks go to:
Thanks go to: Graphical House, Aly Barr,
and especially to our guest artist Marc Baines.